TRACING
YOUR ANCESTORS

A pedigree was once the sign of noble birth
and distinguished ancestry, but now the
fascinating hobby of 'ancestor hunting' is
popular at all levels of society. In this
fascinating book Mr. Camp, who is
Director of Research at the Society of
Genealogists and has edited several works
on the subject, describes the sources by
which you can build up your own pedigree
without any knowledge of your family or
its history. All you require is your own
birth certificate. Armed with this it is
possible to trace your 'family tree' back
as much as three or four hundred years.

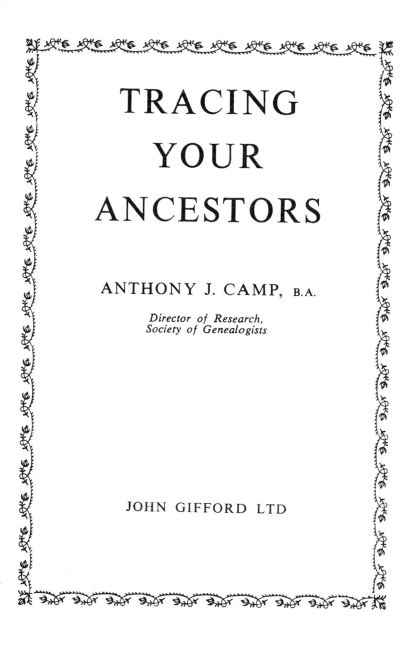

TRACING YOUR ANCESTORS

ANTHONY J. CAMP, B.A.

Director of Research,
Society of Genealogists

JOHN GIFFORD LTD

First Published 1964
Reprinted 1966
New revised edition 1970
Reprinted 1972
Reprinted 1979
©W. & G. Foyle Ltd., 1964

JOHN GIFFORD LTD
125 CHARING CROSS ROAD
LONDON, W.C.2.

ISBN 0 7071 0461 0

Printed in Great Britain by
Thomson Litho Ltd, East Kilbride, Scotland

Contents

Acknowledgments

THE EXECUTIVE COMMITTEE of the Society of Genealogists has kindly allowed me, as Director of Research, to write this introduction to genealogical research, but I should make it clear that any opinion I have expressed herein is entirely personal and does not necessarily represent the official view of the Society.

I am also indebted to the Society of Genealogists and to one of its Vice-Presidents, Sir Anthony Wagner, K.C.V.O., D. Litt., Garter Principal King of Arms, for permission to quote the passage on page 11 from the latter's lecture to the Society on the occasion of its Jubilee in 1961, *Genealogy and the Common Man*.

The Secretary of the Church Commissioners has kindly given me permission to quote the passage on page 23 from the Explanatory Notes to the Parochial Fees Order, 1962, regarding the searching of Parish Registers.

My thanks are also due to Mrs. D. H. Currer Briggs of Leeds and to Noel Currer-Briggs of Taynton for permission to reproduce on the cover part of a pedigree compiled by them and written by Miss Claire G. M. Evans, F.S.G., of Herstmonceux.

My great friend J. W. M. Phillips has once again given me much assistance in the preparation of this book and his practical experience of research in England has prompted him to make many suggestions which add considerably to any value this work may have.

A.J.C.

Walkern Lodge,
Stevenage.

Introduction

OVER the last half century England's population has increased more than in any other previous period of fifty years. This increase has been accompanied by a movement of families which began almost two centuries ago with the drift from the country to the town. This movement has naturally led to a weakening of those ties which formerly existed between families and their original homes, particularly so when this movement spread beyond the seas to the colonies. After about three generations, or perhaps a little more than a hundred years, a natural curiosity arises as to this place of origin, coupled, in the case of those families which went abroad, with a certain pride in the emigrant ancestor and some inquisitiveness as to the reasons which prompted him to leave.

This curiosity amongst Americans in particular is well known to us. Emigration to that country being well under way by the middle of the seventeenth century this interest in their homeland ancestry has existed since the early days of the last century. Today it coincides with a similar interest in England itself, following the general movements at home and the uncertainty of the times which have led some to look for ' roots ' in the more settled age of their ancestors and others to obtain that symbol of status which a pedigree was generally considered to afford.

Perhaps one of these reasons is subconsciously prompting you to read this book. For your pains you may well be called ' fools with long memories ', but you might answer that we are all ' omnibuses in which our ancestors ride ', and not to know who our passengers are shows little gratitude for those who have made us the heirs of so many ages. If, on the other hand, you are planning to claim some vast inheritance which great-aunt-Mary mentioned on her death-bed, or a title which ' rightfully ' belonged

9

to your grandfather, I would advise you to see a solicitor and have a few words about the Limitation Act of 1939 and the Lords' Humble Address to the Crown in 1927 before embarking on further expense.* There is no need to be frightened of unearthing a dubious ancestor as you will almost certainly not search the court records which would reveal this, at least for the last 150 years, and surely you can live down even a major criminal after such a length of time. As regards illegitimacy, you will have to be prepared for this. I doubt if there are many families which do not have at least one illegitimate child amongst their ancestors. He has just as many ancestors as any other child and, after all, no doubt you would be very proud of him if he turned out to be the son of a Royal duke.

Contrary to common belief the pedigrees of all people with English ancestry are not filed away in endless drawers in that proverbial heaven of the ancestor hunter, Somerset House. There they do indeed have the records of General Registration of Births, Marriages and Deaths in England and Wales since July 1837 and the records of some English persons abroad, but these entries are in no way connected together and each has to be hunted out separately through the indexes and pieced together as described in the first chapter of this book.

Before rushing to Somerset House you can obviously save yourself a great deal of trouble and expense by quizzing your oldest relations and ransacking any family papers you may have, although I am working on the assumption that you have neither. For the first hundred or so years of your pedigree from the present day the dates of events on it are much more important than the places (unless you have a common name) and if these are vague in any way it is safest to start with a known date however recent this may be and work from there to the unknown, reconstructing the events in your ancestor's life as you go, his birth, baptism, education, marriage, career, death and burial, and

* By the Limitation Act funds administered by the Crown cannot be claimed after a lapse of more than twelve years. Funds held by the Supreme Court to which no valid claim has yet been made rarely exceed £150, but a list of these ' Dormant Funds ' may be consulted, without fee, in the Eastern Corridor, Ground Floor, of the Royal Courts of Justice, Strand, London, W.C.2. As a result of the Royal Assent to the Humble Address of the Lords no claim can be made to a peerage which has been in abeyance more than 100 years.

then seeing how he comes into contact with his neighbours through litigation and with the government through the census, military service, taxation, elections, etc. all of which leave records.

There are four factors, in the words of the present Garter King of Arms, which above all govern success or failure in tracing pedigrees: 'These are status, name, continuity and record. If a family is of eminent status, has a rare surname and distinctive Christian names; maintains continuity with its past, by living in, or owning land in, the same place, pursuing the same occupation or otherwise; and finally if the relevant records happen to be well preserved; then indeed we may hope for success. But in proportion as one or more of these requisites is lacking, we must brace ourselves to encounter difficulties'. Thus it will be seen that a nineteenth century labouring family may possibly be traced back to the sixteen hundreds if it stayed in the same place and the Parish Registers still survive, yet a relatively landed family may not be easily traced beyond 1800 because of constant movement and the loss of records. Before the sixteenth century the tracing of a pedigree depends almost entirely on the ownership of land, the descent of which is recorded in the Manor Rolls of the thousands of Manors which existed throughout England, but these records have only haphazardly survived.

Most families must thus content themselves with a pedigree which goes back about three, or at the most, four hundred years. An authentic pedigree of a family of the poorer classes which goes back earlier than this is a great rarity and it is well to remember that only two English families can, with certainty, trace their pedigrees in the male line to a Saxon ancestor before 1066 (Arden and Berkeley), and that *no one* can trace a similar line to a person who definitely fought at the Battle of Hastings although a few can trace a genuine male descent from a Domesday tenant of 1086 (notably Fitzgerald, Carew, Gresley, and possibly St. John from tenants-in-chief, and Shirley and Wrottesley from subtenants).

If there is reason to suppose that a pedigree of the family has already been drawn up there are several things that you can do. All printed pedigrees of more than three generations were indexed by G. W. Marshall in 1903 in a book entitled *The Genealogist's Guide* and this was supplemented and continued by J. B. Whitmore in *A Genealogical Guide* (1953). Many of the books mentioned in these volumes and in T. R. Thomson's *Catalogue of British Family Histories* (1935) will be found in the Library of the Society of Genealogists which is described in Chapter Eight. Also at the Society is a large collection of manuscript family histories which genealogists have deposited over the past fifty years on the completion of their work. If the family was armigerous it is quite possible that a pedigree has been recorded at the College of Arms, described in Chapter Ten.

However, as with the majority of families, the work you do will probably be the first ever on your family, and we now begin on that presumption with your own birth, remembering that when you have completed your task (or grown tired of it), you will deposit the result of your work in one of the above repositories.

CHAPTER ONE

Back to 1837

FOR THE SAKE of simplicity in this Chapter I am going
to presume that you know nothing at all about your ancestors
and do not even have a copy of your own birth certificate, but
that you know when and roughly where you were born.

If you go to Somerset House in the Strand, London, W.C.2,
and turn left under the colonnade, an attendant will show you
how to fill in a form of Application for a Birth Certificate. On
this you are asked to state your name, date and place of birth,
and particulars of your parents. These latter will not help you to
find the correct entry in the indexes but may be used by the
officials when copying the certificate to check that you have
found the right one. The indexes, which are to be found in galleries
around the room, are divided quarterly, March, June, September
and December. Thus all the births registered between 1st January
and 31st March fall in the March Quarter, those registered between
1st April and 30th June fall in the June Quarter, and so on, remembering that a birth on, say, 28th March may not be registered
until April. Armed with the exact date of your own birth you should
have no trouble in finding the correct entry, but if the name is a
common one you have only the Registration District to identify it,
for the entries in the indexes of births are simply as follows:
You then enter the appropriate quarter and year, registration
district, volume and page on your form and return to the

Surname and Christian Names	District	Volume	Page
Walker, John Henry	Wolverhampton	XVII	272

counter. On paying 8s. for a certified copy of the entry (you can obtain no information from Somerset House except in the form of a certificate) you are asked if you can collect the copy (it is usually ready the next day), or if you want it sent to you. If the latter is the case you are asked to address an envelope to yourself with no further charge. When the certificate is being copied the details on it are checked with the known details on your form and if these do not tally your 6s. is refunded.

The birth certificate will show the name of your father and the maiden name of your mother. The next step is to look for their marriage. You cannot jump to the birth of your father as you will not know either a rough date or the name of his father until you have obtained his marriage certificate. The marriages (and deaths) are on the right hand side of the entrance at Somerset House. A similar procedure is followed as for births but the indexes contain both the names of the brides and grooms. Thus if your mother's name is less common than your father's you can search under this, working back from the date of your own birth or that of a known elder brother or sister. Once you find a likely looking reference you can check under the other party's name to see if both have the same reference, if not then you continue searching. This cross checking is not as easy as it sounds if the names are both common and fall in different volumes of the indexes (of which there may be several for each quarter). Remember that a marriage may take place twenty or thirty years before the birth of the youngest child or very shortly before (and in some cases after!) the birth of the eldest.

The marriage certificate will show your father's age and his father's name. From this you can calculate your father's approximate date of birth and repeat the procedure, looking for his birth, then for the marriage of your grandparents, the birth of your grandfather, the marriage of your great-grandparents, and so on.

The ages given on Marriage Certificates may be exact, but they may say 'over 21' or 'of full age', 'minor', or '21 years' usually meaning twenty-one and over, and due allowance must be made in each case. If the birth entry cannot be found, not more than sixteen years should be deducted from the date of marriage and a search made from that time backwards in the indexes.

There should be little difficulty in tracing the appropriate birth

entries unless your name is a common one. If the latter is the
case and you are searching, say, for the birth of a John Smith
within the short period July 1879 to July 1880 (he having given his
age as twenty-seven when he married in July 1907) there will probably be many possible entries, even taking into account the fact
that he was probably born not far from where he married and spent
the rest of his life. Taking the more likely ones first you can
have these checked by the officials at Somerset House by filling
up a special form with all the likely references from the indexes.
The officials will then check each of these in turn against the
filed certificates using the name of the father, which you must
supply, until the correct entry is found. You will then be charged
2s. for every reference checked.

A little knowledge of human frailties is helpful as ages on
marriage certificates are often incorrect, even more so on death
certificates where the informant is not a member of the family;
additional christian names are often assumed in later life and do
not appear on the birth certificate, and if a lady has been married
twice she may when registering the births of children by her
second husband say that she is ' Mary Smith formerly Jones '
when Jones is in fact her maiden name and not the name by
which she was secondly married thus making a search for this
latter marriage more difficult if not impossible.

The records of births, marriages, and deaths at Somerset House
go back to 1st July 1837 and registration has been compulsory
since that time. Some births in the early days escaped registration as did a very few deaths, but marriage registration has always
been complete. For the purposes of tracing a pedigree the records
of deaths are little used and entries, in any case, are often difficult
to identify as the indexes do not give the age at death until 1866.
It will be seen from the above that one would probably need to
make several visits to Somerset House on successive days to trace
a pedigree back to 1837, but certificates will be supplied by post
if exact details are given. The cost of certificates, when application is made by post, is 13s., which includes the handling charge. The
illustrations in the Appendix (p. 76) show the amount of information to be found on English birth, death and marriage certificates.

There are now no charges for making searches in the indexes at
Somerset House, and if your name is fairly uncommon you may
care to make a general search of the indexes and list out all entries

of your surname. Such an undertaking can be very arduous and will probably take at least five full days, but can be very rewarding. The indexes are open to public search daily from 9.30 a.m. to 4.30 p.m. (Saturdays to 12.30 p.m.).

If your family consistently lived in one place it may be easier to do your searching through the local registry office, the isolation of entries and the identification of the brothers and sisters of your ancestors being facilitated by indexes covering a much smaller area. At Somerset House the indexes before 1866 are hand-written in heavy parchment volumes and searching there is not a job for the sick or elderly.

CHAPTER TWO

The Census Returns

E VER SINCE 1801 a Census of the population of England
and Wales has been taken every ten years (with the exception
of 1941). Those for 1801, 1811, 1821 and 1831 which contained
only statistical information were destroyed, but those for 1841,
1851 and 1861 are now housed by the Public Record Office in the
Land Registry Building, Portugal Street, London, W.C.2., and are
open to public inspection although a Reader's Ticket is needed
(see Chapter Seven).

Having determined from either a birth or marriage registered
at Somerset House where your ancestors were living in the above
years the Census Returns can be used to find where the various
members of the family were born before 1837 thus indicating
which parish registers should be searched to carry the family
further back, as well as indicating other members of the family
in the same household and living in the neighbourhood.

The Census records are not indexed in any way by name but
are arranged parish by parish and the order of the families therein follows the streets house by house as the enumerator made his
rounds. The forms, which were distributed before the night on
which the Census was to be made, were collected and copied on
to further forms which were bound into volumes, the sections
of the volumes being preceded by a description of the area
covered. Several of these volumes in a box are termed a ' bundle '
and each bundle has its own reference number which is easily
found in the indexes. The indexes are arranged alphabetically by
parish but there are other lists arranged by bundle showing the areas
covered by each bundle, these latter being particularly useful for
finding the Returns of hamlets and other small places. There are
street indexes (not necessarily complete) for London and some other

large towns for the 1851 Census only but searches in other large towns can be very lengthy although the use of a contemporary Directory (see Chapter eight) may help to identify the particular street or area required.

The 1841 Returns (taken on the night of 7th June) do not contain such valuable information as the later ones. The persons in each household are listed with their occupations but the relationship between them is not shown. The ages up to fifteen are supposed to be correct and those after fifteen have been reduced to the nearest multiple of five, e.g. twenty-four is reduced to twenty and twenty-nine to twenty-five. With regard to the places of birth, 'Y(es)' stands for those born in the county of their residence, 'N(o)' for those not born in the same county, 'S' for those in Scotland, 'I' for those in Ireland, and 'F' for those in foreign parts. Thus a typical entry is as follows, the lists being usually in pencil and sometimes very faded:

George	Williams	35	Ag(ricultural) Lab(ourer)	Y
Frances	do	30		N
George	do	12		Y
Emma	do	9		Y
Jane	do	6		Y
Harriet Peters		15	F(emale) S(ervant)	Y

The stroke after Jane indicates the end of one family, the double stroke after Harriet the end of the household.

The information contained in the 1851 Returns (taken on the night of 30th March) and in those for 1861 (8th April) and later includes the relationship of each person to the head of the household, their exact ages, whether they are married or not, fuller details of their occupations (e.g. 'Farmer of 250 acres employing 4 men and 2 boys'), and most important of all their exact places of birth, county and parish, or the country abroad, e.g.

George	Williams	Head	Mar	47	Ag.lab	Writtle, Essex
Frances	do	Wife	Mar	42	Laundress	Ardley, Herts.
Emma	do	Dau	Unm	19		Writtle, Essex
Jane	do	Dau	Unm	16		do do

Such entries are written in ink on light blue paper.

These Returns are of obvious value. A young married person

found in the 1851 Census, say, in London, giving his birth place at Basingstoke may well be found in the 1841 Returns for Basingstoke with his presumed parents who may then themselves be found in the 1851 Returns. The birthplace of elderly members of the family are of particular importance as they can often carry one back immediately to the 1780's and the place of origin of the family before it moved, along with so many others, at the end of the eighteenth and the beginning of the nineteenth century.

If a person was away from home on the night of the Census he, of course, will not appear and may well be very difficult to find unless he is in the near neighbourhood. The younger members of a family may be acting as servants in the local farmhouse, or staying as apprentices with the local baker or as scholars at the nearest school if they are not at home. Those who cannot be found in 1851 may, with luck, of course, be there in 1861 or vice versa.

In cases of particular difficulty or when the name is so common as to make searches at Somerset House almost impossible it might be worth having the later Census Returns searched. Those from 1871 onwards are in the care of the Registrar General at Somerset House and are not open to public inspection but the officials there may undertake searches under certain conditions. A fee of 30s. must be prepaid and covers a search of one address for one family, the applicant giving an undertaking that the information obtained will not be used in litigation, stating his relationship to the family enquired about and the views of any other descendants, and also giving the exact address to be searched.

It should be remembered that the information in the Census Returns, like that found in Somerset House, is simply what was stated by the informant and if that person was uncertain of some details he could only state what was true to the best of his knowledge. In some areas where resistance to the numbering of the people was strong, particularly in the West Country, it may be that incorrect information was purposely given. It is the age and place of birth that usually suffers but if your ancestor can be found in all three available returns you may at least hope that the information he gave was correct on one occasion.

CHAPTER THREE

Parish Registers and other Parish Records

H AVING discovered your earliest known ancestors in the records of the 1851 Census you will now know the exact places of birth of some of them before 1837. You must now proceed to search the Parish Registers of that place.

Parish Registers

Registers of baptisms, marriages and burials, in every parish throughout England and Wales, were first ordered to be kept in September 1538 and in a few places are complete from that time to the present day. In 1597 the registers were ordered to be copied into parchment volumes and if the earlier register does survive it is usually in the form of this copy of the original although the paper volume has occasionally survived as well. In many parishes the registers only begin at 1597, the earlier copy (if it was ever made) having been lost. In 1645 the ministers were charged to make note of all births, as well as baptisms, marriages and burials, and in 1653 during the Commonwealth the registers were taken out of their hands and given to laymen who were to be called the 'Parish Registers'. The men appointed were often illiterate and in a large number of parishes no entries appear from that date until 1660 (when the task was returned to the clergy on the restoration of the Monarchy), the register either having never been kept, having been lost or having stayed in private hands. In some cases where the register was conscientiously kept the entries are particularly full in the information they give. The ' Registers ' were not ordered to keep records of baptisms so where records do survive they are usually of births for that period. No marriage could take place without a certificate from the Register that he had published banns on ' three successive Lord's days ' after morning service in church or on three successive market days in the nearest market place, the parties being then married by a Justice of the Peace. Because of the doubtful legitimacy of the children of these marriages they were legalized by Act of Parliament in 1660.

The next Act affecting Parish Registers was passed in 1667 and was devised to promote the woollen trade, providing that ' no corpse of any person . . . shall be buried in . . . anything whatsoever . . . other than what is made of sheep's wool only ' or a heavy fine paid. An affidavit had to be brought to the Minister within eight days to this effect and this was usually noted in the burial register or in a separate volume kept for the purpose. The Act was more strictly enforced in 1678 but in most parishes it had long fallen into disuse before it was repealed in 1814. It is of some interest as the person bringing the affidavit was often a relation of the deceased.

In 1694 a tax was placed on births, marriages and deaths and for a short period the births of Dissenters came thus to be recorded because a penalty of £100 could be incurred by the Incumbent for neglect. In many cases, however, there was a sharp decline in the number of entries recorded to save the tax. The Act was only in force for five years and when this period expired no further action was taken, the registration of births as opposed to baptisms being generally discontinued. A similar Act passed in 1783 caused an even greater decline because it was based directly on the number of entries in the register. This was repealed in 1794.

So far in the history of Parish Registers no regulation had been made as to the amount of information to be recorded about each event, but in 1754 a register of printed forms was introduced for the recording of marriages. This Act, which is commonly known as Lord Hardwicke's Marriage Act, was primarily concerned with clandestine marriages for which no banns had been read or licence obtained but which were valid and indissoluble although the parties and the celebrant could incur legal penalties. The Act declared all marriages contracted after 25th March 1754 to be void unless they were solemnized in a church or chapel by licence or after the publication of banns. The banns were recorded at the back of the marriage register or in a separate register, and sometimes contained more information as to the place of origin of the parties than the entry of the marriage itself. This Act, being limited to England and Wales, was easily evaded by going to Scotland or the Channel Islands where consent before witnesses was still sufficient to constitute a legal marriage. It did not apply to the Quakers or Jews.

In 1812 an Act provided that all future registers of baptisms and burials were to be kept in books provided by the king's printers according to a uniform scheme and these volumes are the same as those used at the present time, although the form of the marriage registers was changed again in 1837 and is thereafter the same as that illustrated on page 76. The baptismal and burial register entries after 1812 are illustrated on pages 74-5.

Before 1754 it is quite common to find entries of baptisms, marriages and burials mixed together in the same volume. The practice of recording the entries in Latin fortunately had died out by about 1620 but, as stated above, the actual amount of information varied considerably before the introduction of the printed-form registers. A baptism may simply say ' Mary Brown baptized ', ' The daughter of John Brown baptized ' or, on the other hand, ' Mary third daughter of John Brown, plumber of this parish, by Ann his wife the daughter of William Smith glazier of Frome in the county of Somerset baptized '. Although the names of god-parents were ordered to be recorded in 1555 entries are rarely found. Baptisms generally took place within a month of birth but several years can elapse between the two events. Before 1754 marriages are usually recorded as ' John Brown and Ann Smith married ' but may sometimes give their places of residence and the parents' names. Burials frequently give the occupation and occasionally the age of the deceased as well as the parentage if it was a child; in a few cases the cause of death is also included. The age and occupation is regularly given from 1812 onwards as can be seen from the illustration on page 75.

Although registers are thus supposed to have been kept since 1538 only about one in fifteen is extant from that time and many do not begin until late in the next century. The early provisions for their safe-keeping were quite inadequate and over the years (and to this day) registers have been lost or misused. In most cases they are still in the hands of the clergy who are legally entitled to fees for searches in them, but in some cases have been deposited in County or Diocesan Record Offices. The clergy are legally obliged 'at all reasonable times' to allow searches to be made in any register book in their keeping, but they are not legally bound to permit the photographing of registers, to supply certificates on postal application (though normally this is done on payment of the appropriate fee), or to make searches on behalf of an enquirer (though they may consent to do this for such remuneration as may be agreed).

The fees for register searching are now fixed in the case of baptisms and burials by the Parochial Fees Order of 1962, being 3s. for the first year and 1s. 6d. for every additional year, a certified copy of the entry being 5s. In the case of marriages the fees were fixed by a Departmental Order in 1952, being 1s. 6d. for the first year, 9d. for every additional year and 3s. 9d. for a certified copy. The co-operation given by the clergy varies enormously but many are willing though not obliged to accept a compounding fee for a general search of the registers which is usually based on the amount of time taken. It should be remembered that in some parishes the number of entries is such that it may take several hours very tiring work to search just three or four years in the register (at St. Pancras, for instance, there were sometimes as many as 80 baptisms *a day*) and the clergyman cannot be expected to supervise you in his vestry for such a lengthy period. On the other hand you cannot expect him to leave you alone with such valuable records (although he might do so to a professional searcher well known in the area) or to produce them at a moment's notice. You may think that this constitutes a good reason for them to be deposited in a local Record Office, but that is another matter.

It should be remembered that before 1752 the ecclesiastical and legal year began on 25th March and an entry in a Parish Register for, say, 10th February 1698 should be shown on a pedigree or in other references as 10th February 1698/9 to show that the event actually took place in the historical year 1699.

At the time of the 1831 Census a return was called for of all existing registers up to 1812 and this was printed in 1833 as *The Parish Register Abstract* forming a list of all the then known registers and the periods they covered. It has never been superseded and remains the standard list although obviously some registers have since disappeared or been destroyed and a few have since been discovered. One or two counties, e.g. Essex, Somerset and Hampshire, have published more detailed and recent lists of their registers.

Fortunately it is not always necessary to consult the original registers, a number having been copied and some printed. The largest collection of transcripts is at the Society of Genealogists (see Chapter eight) and many Public Libraries have other copies both manuscript and printed, the latter being mainly the work either of local Parish Register Societies, such as those for Lancashire, Yorkshire, Devon and Cornwall, or of Phillimore & Co. Ltd. who have published some hundreds of marriage registers. These copies are not collectively indexed apart from about 7,000,000 marriages and some burials in the London area, both of these indexes being at the Society of Genealogists. *A Catalogue of Parish Registers in the Possession of the Society of Genealogists* was published in 1968. The Society also edited a list of those in other repositories and in private hands called *A National Index of Parish Register Copies* (1939), a new edition of which is in the process of being published in several volumes.

Bishops Transcripts

In addition to maintaining their registers the Incumbents were ordered in 1597 to send annual copies of the entries in their registers to the bishop of the diocese (in some cases they were sent to the Archdeacon as well) but this was so sporadically carried out and so little care was taken of the returns when they were received that many are now missing and in most dioceses are far from complete until the early eighteenth century, although there are usually good runs after about 1750. In the Diocese of London it was 'not the custom' to send in such returns. They usually continue well into the last century and in some cases into this, the Canon apparently never having been changed. They are often a valuable addition to the Parish Register in that they help to fill gaps and sometimes contain detail which was omitted in the registers. Like the copies of the early registers before 1597, the burial affidavit books and the banns books they should always be consulted and cross-checked for that little clue or extra piece of information which may indicate a family's place of origin before it moved into the parish you are concerned with. The Bishops Transcripts and Marriage Licences which we discuss next are now either in the appropriate Diocesan or County Record Office.

Marriage Licences

Many marriages took place not by banns but by licence which enabled (as it does today) the parties to marry either without the delay occasioned by the reading of banns, or if both parties were away from their normal place of residence. The licence was normally obtained from the bishop of the diocese in which the parties resided, but if they lived in different dioceses they should have applied to the Vicar-General of the Archbishop of either the Province of Canterbury or York and if in different Provinces to the Archbishop of Canterbury's Master of Faculties. However, certain other minor ecclesiastical officials issued licences for persons within their jurisdictions. The allegations (i.e., statements) made and bonds given in order to obtain a licence were filed and should give the names of the parties, their descriptions, ages, parishes, as well as parentage if the parties were under age and had to have their parents' consent, and the place or places where the marriage could take place. Some of these have been printed and a few others copied in manuscript by the Society of Genealogists. The originals, as stated above, are either in the appropriate Diocesan or County Record Office. Those issued by the Archbishop of Canterbury are at Lambeth Palace Library and those by the Archbishop of York at the Borthwick Institute, St. Anthony's Hall, York.

Monumental Inscriptions

Before passing on to the other parochial records it is certainly worth noting any monumental inscriptions in the church or churchyard which relate to your family, for the information given on them so often adds to that in the registers, particularly as to age and exact date of death, and sometimes, to the place of origin of the deceased. Many have been copied and are to be found in public libraries and there may well be a copy amongst the church records together with a plan of the churchyard.

The Parish Chest

The church chest often contains much else of interest to the genealogist and if your ancestors lived in a parish for some time it is most important that you should see as much of this as possible. It is here that the records of the really poor appear, for the churchwardens and overseers, whose accounts may begin before the parish registers, were responsible for the poor of the parish and those who after a lifetime of farm labouring became unable to work were their special problem. Those to whom payments were made are recorded each year: '*Paide Joshif Parker 51 weeks at 1 shils & 6 pence per weeke £3-13-6* ', as well as special purchases for the poor: '*Old Parker a shirt and a paer of stockins 5s. 2d.*' and that final entry: '*Paide for buring Joseph Parker the Charge £1-4-0* ' (Shephall, Herts., 1767). The parish officers were obviously keen to see that no more than necessary should become a charge on the parish, and persons entering it were required to bring with them a certificate stating that they were settled in their old parishes and that the authorities there would receive them back if the need should arise. These settlement certificates which were established by Act of Parliament in 1697 are often to be found in the parish chest or the particulars from them copied into the parish registers. Unfortunately as they became out of date they were often thrown away, but where they do survive they provide invaluable evidence of the movement of a family from one parish to another. Earlier acts had given similar powers to the churchwardens and entries like the following are often encountered: '*Grigory Randall born at Teuxbury in Glostershire was taken vagrant in the parish of Stone (in the Isle of Oxney, Kent) April 18 1620 and was whipped and sent away according to the Statute*'.

Details of the local workhouse and its inmates would also be recorded after the Act establishing them in 1722 together with the appointment of their masters. The fear of the poor being harboured led to lists of newly erected cottages being included, for these were illegal between 1588 and 1752 unless they had four acres of freehold land allotted to them, and the care of the sick poor led to the appointment of parish doctors and also perhaps to the establishment of a Pest House. The number of illegitimate children became such a charge on some parishes that the vestry was more than interested in ascertaining the father and placing the charge on him or making him marry the mother: '*Charges expended on Joseph Newton and his getting Widow Moss with child and then marrying her £4-6s.-6d.*' (Stevenage, Herts., 1730).

Pauper children were also the care of the churchwarden who had to see them put to work and if they were placed as apprentices the indenture (or contract of service) would also be kept in the parish chest and a note made of the cost in the accounts.

To pay for all this a poor-rate was levied and the rate books of the parish, if they have survived, may give a valuable indication of the length of a family's stay in a parish together with some idea of their status which can be reckoned from the amount paid.

Other documents usually to be found in parish churches are fully described in W. E. Tate's interesting book *The Parish Chest* (3rd ed. 1969) although it is only fair to say that many of you will certainly be disappointed by the results of the spring-cleaning efforts of former clergy in the parishes in which you are interested.

CHAPTER FOUR

Wills and Administrations

WILLS and administrations have been recorded from an early period in English history and regular series exist in some places from the thirteenth century. Naturally not everyone left wills but where they do exist they are invaluable in the amount of biographical information they give and the relationships mentioned. The possibility that any one of your ancestors left a will should certainly be investigated.

After 1858 this is a fairly easy matter. In that year the Principal Probate Registry and its system of District Registries was established and copies of *all* wills proved and administrations granted since then have been sent from the District Registries to the Principal Registry where a yearly index is compiled. A search fee of 1s. is charged for a search in the indexes at the Principal Registry which is situated at Somerset House directly across the courtyard from the main Strand entrance. This fee also includes the production of any will or administration which you may then read and take short extracts from. Photostat copies can also be supplied at a rate of 2s. per page.

If your name is not too common it is again helpful to make a general search in these indexes which give more detail than the indexes of deaths. If you are looking for a person's date of death after 1858 and there is a good likelihood that he or she left a will then it is often much quicker and cheaper to search the Will indexes than those of the Deaths. It should perhaps be pointed out here that before the Married Women's Property Act of 1882 most married women would have had no property to bequeath and thus did not make wills, but wills could always be left by widows and spinsters and are often remarkable for the number of relatives and family possessions that they mention.

28

Before 1858 the probate of wills was a function of about 300 ecclesiastical and minor temporal courts one or more of which had jurisdiction over the place where the testator held land or died. You will soon have to find out under which ecclesiastical jurisdiction your ancestors lived, for this affected them in several ways as we have seen with the issuing of marriage licences and the return of Bishop's Transcripts. Lewis's *Topographical Dictionary* (13 vols., 1840–7) which can be found in many large public libraries will show in which diocese or other jurisdiction any parish fell. The general rule of jurisdiction was that the will of a testator with property (*a*) solely within one archdeaconry could be proved in the court of the archdeacon, (*b*) in two such archdeaconries, in the court of the bishop, (*c*) in two bishoprics in the court of the appropriate archbishop, (*d*) in the two archbishoprics, then in the senior, Canterbury. Besides these general jurisdictions there were also a large number of minor ecclesiastical officials, as well as some corporations and manor courts which had the right to prove the wills of persons who had property solely within the small areas of their jurisdictions. All these courts are detailed county by county in *Wills and Their Whereabouts* by Anthony J. Camp (1963) which also shows where the original records are deposited.

The wills proved in the court of the Archbishop of Canterbury (known as the Prerogative Court of Canterbury and abbreviated to P.C.C.) begin in 1383 and are deposited in the Department of Literary Enquiry at Somerset House (together with those Principal Probate Registry Wills which are more than 100 years old) where they may be seen at the usual charge of 1s. each or free if a ticket is obtained by applying with suitable references to the President of the Probate, Divorce and Admiralty Division of the High Court of Justice, Somerset House, London, W.C.2.

This court (P.C.C.) which had jurisdiction throughout England and Wales and which theoretically should only have proved wills relating to people who had property in two dioceses or in both provinces, did in fact prove many wills of persons who held property in only one jurisdiction and thus searches should be made there first. The wills of persons who died at sea, abroad, or in the colonies and had some property in England were usually proved in this court. The indexes of wills proved have been printed up to 1700 (mainly in the British Records Society Index

Library series) and there are manuscript calendars up to 1852 at the Literary Department, the short period 1853-7 being covered by an official printed index. During the Commonwealth (1653-60) it was the only court which functioned and the printed indexes covering that period give an excellent idea as to the distribution of any given surname at that time. The Literary Department and Principal Probate Registry are open Monday to Friday, 10 a.m. to 4 p.m.

The wills proved in the Prerogative Court of York (abbreviated to P.C.Y.) from 1389 to 1858 are deposited at the Borthwick Institute of Historical Research, St. Anthony's Hall, York, and indexes up to 1688 have been printed by the Yorkshire Archaeological Society.

Wills proved in the other courts are generally now deposited in the County Record Office most nearly concerned with the area of the court's jurisdiction. Indexes for these have not usually been printed after 1700, but there are a few exceptions. Full details of exactly what records have been printed are given in *Wills and Their Whereabouts* from which you can easily tell which courts are the likely ones to have records of your ancestors and which records have survived.

The original will was normally filed, copied into a large register and noted in a Probate Act Book, a Probate Copy being handed to the executors as their authorization to act. For the P.C.C. it is usually the Register Copy which is produced to enquirers, but the original can be seen on payment of a further fee of 1s. When a person did not leave a Will and his heirs felt that they needed some legal authority to settle the affairs of the deceased they applied for letters of administration. An entry was made in the Administration Book (e.g. '*Administration of the goods of John Adams late of the parish of St. James Westminster in the Co. of Middlesex batchelor deceased granted to William Adams of the parish of St. Paul Hammersmith the brother of the said deceased being first sworn*') and the administrator made a bond, which was also filed, promising to administer faithfully. Up to about 1700 it was usual with Wills and almost invariable with Administrations to submit an Inventory of the goods of the deceased and this was usually filed with the Administration Bond or Original Will. An Inventory will list all the goods of the deceased in some detail from '*In the parlour, two bedds and bedding, one chest of drawers, two other chests, one table, and four chairs £5'*, to *'Poultry in the yard 5s'* (Thomas Hardy, Goxhill, Lincs. 1721), and will give an excellent idea of the social condition of your ancestor.

Most record offices are able to supply fairly cheap photostatic copies of any of these classes of document but as explained in Chapter Nine they cannot be expected to make lengthy searches for particular wills and may well refer you to a locally resident record searcher who will undertake the search for you for a fee which should, of course, be agreed beforehand. If you obtain the reference to a will from a printed index or can at least give the exact date of death then the easiest and often quickest procedure is to ask for a photostat which you can then puzzle out at your leisure, for the writing used by the clerks in copying the wills is not always easily read and the Act Books are usually in Latin. Because of this it is sometimes more convenient to have photostats made of the original will if it survives than of the register copy as the former is often in a clearer hand and in any case is of more personal interest as it has the signature or mark of your ancestor. If you employ a professional searcher he will either make a full abstract of all the details in the will or just a 'genealogical abstract' of the persons mentioned.

Wills are one of the most important sources of information which shed light on the movement of families and prove connections between families of the same name living in different parishes and you will soon find that it is useful to have extracts of all the Wills of your surname proved in the local courts and often, if the name is not too common, in the Prerogative Courts as well. It may be that you will *have* to do this to discover where your ancestors came from before appearing in a particular parish, and remember it is not and never has been only people with property and money who leave wills. They, more than any other record, can breathe life and character into the dullest ancestor.

NOTE: In May, 1970, all the records of the Prerogative Court of Canterbury, 1383–1858, were moved from the Department of Literary Enquiry at Somerset House to the Public Record Office, Chancery Lane, where they are available to the public without charge. The Wills after 1858 remain at Somerset House.

CHAPTER FIVE

Nonconformists and other 'Non-parochials'

T HE RELIGION of one's ancestors is not a thing that affects one genealogically back to 1837, for all births, deaths and marriages since that date, as we have seen, are registered at Somerset House. Indeed, it is only the records of marriages there that give a clue to the religion of the parties unless it can be gleaned from the type of Christian name used.

Before 1837, however, the records of those persons who did not belong to the Church of England form classes of their own which have particular problems. Parish Registers had been instituted at a time when all Englishmen professed the same religion, but when religious uniformity ceased to be the law of the land the dissenting bodies kept their own registers which had no legal status in England. This was also the case for a large number of other registers, like those kept at the Foundling Hospitals and the Chapels Royal, which, being 'non-parochial', were not recognized in law.

Religious toleration in this country was unknown before about 1650 but it was not until the Declarations of Indulgence from 1672 onwards, and more so after the Toleration Act of 1689, that Protestant dissenters secured licences for the conduct of worship according to their own consciences in stated places. They had, of course, met together secretly for many years and a very few had kept registers. These registers are mainly of baptisms, though births were recorded where, as among the Quakers, the rite of baptism had been abandoned. After 1754 no marriage could be performed except by a clergyman of the Church of England and this remained the law until 1837 when, incidentally, Registry Offices were introduced. As a result there are very few nonconformist marriage registers, the exceptions being mainly those of the Quakers and Jews who because of the meticulous way in which their marriages had been registered were specially exempted and allowed to marry according to their own rites. Some sects which also declined the use of the parish churchyard, in early days usually the Quakers, provided themselves with burial grounds for which they kept registers and by the end of the eighteenth century many had such grounds, for it was not until 1880 that nonconformist ministers were allowed to perform burial ceremonies in parish churchyards.

In 1837 a Royal Commission was appointed to enquire into the state, custody and authenticity of these 'non-parochial' registers, and to recommend means for their collection and arrangement and legal use and availability. About 6,500 registers were collected, mainly from Baptists, Congregationalists, Presbyterians, Wesleyans and Quakers. The Jews and the majority of Roman Catholics refused to part with their registers and these, together with many of those of the other denominations, remained in the custody of the churches concerned where the majority so retained continue to this day and where enquiry should be made. Those registers which were sent in were generally pronounced to be authentic and admissible for legal purposes by Act of Parliament and a full list of them arranged by counties was printed, *List of the Non-Parochial Registers and Records in the Custody of the Registrar General* (1859). They were transferred in 1961 from Somerset House to the Public Record Office, and they may now be consulted without charge at The Land Registry Building, Portugal Street, London, W.C.2. The registers relate mainly to the eighteenth and the first half of the nineteenth century but some start in the seventeenth and a very few in the sixteenth century.

Before the Quakers surrendered their registers the whole of the 500,000 entries therein were digested into index form. Two copies were made, one of which has been deposited with the local Quarterly Meeting records, the other complete set may be found at the Library of the Society of Friends in Friends House, Euston Road, N.W.1, together with a large amount of other Quaker material.

The dissenters had long recognized that some more centralized and regular form of registration of the births of their children was needed and in 1742 a Registry was started in London at the library founded by the Presbyterian Dr. Daniel Williams in Red

Cross Street, Cripplegate, births being registered on receipt of declarations made by witnesses of the event. Although originally limited to dissenters within 12 miles of London the register does include entries from other areas, for being kept with great care it was used by dissenters of all denominations particularly those for whom no provision was made by other registers. The Registers from ' Dr. Williams' Library ' were amongst those authenticated in 1840 and are now in the Land Registry Building as are those of Bunhill Fields (1713-1852) the chief Nonconformist burial ground for the London district.

Apart from registers most of the dissenting churches kept minute books and church rolls recording their membership, some in considerable detail, which survive at the churches concerned or, if these are defunct, at the various denominational head-quarters, or their Historical Societies, or the District Associations. Most of them also published some form of magazine which are useful for their obituary notices, memoirs, and notices of marriages and deaths, the *Baptist Magazine* (from 1809), the *Congregational Magazine* (from 1818), and the Methodist *Arminian Magazine* (from 1778) called the *Methodist Magazine* after 1798 and the *Wesleyan Methodist Magazine* after 1822, being examples. Details of ministers may usually be found in the early Baptist *Handbooks*, Congregational *Year Books*, and Methodist *Minutes*, sets of which are generally to be found at the denominational headquarters or theological colleges (where these exist) and in the possession of local Association Secretaries.

Roman Catholics having suffered considerable intolerance before 1829 are most difficult to trace. They were excluded from the benefits of the Toleration Act in 1689 and were not allowed their own places of worship until 1832. Nevertheless they met together and sometimes kept secret registers of their baptisms and marriages from a much earlier period. For their marriages to be legal they had to be solemnized in the parish church but this did not prevent them from going through a second ceremony in private. For their burials, however, they may well have had to submit, like the Anabaptists, to being ' hurled into the ground ' (Toddington, Beds., 1728), or to being treated as having died excommunicate as they were in the reign of Queen Elizabeth I, or, at the best, the Church of England ceremony with entry in the Parish Register as a ' Papist '. The Catholic Record Society has published many of the registers which have survived and the printed volumes are detailed in *Texts and Calendars* by E. L. C. Mullins (1958). Details of Roman Catholics were often reported by the parish clergy to their bishops, and details of their estates had to be registered by the Quarter Sessions (1717), the County Record Offices probably having other material as well. The Recusant Rolls in the Public Record Office form a useful register of the more 'notorious' of the Catholics in the period from Elizabeth to William and Mary.

Jewish ancestors are not so difficult to trace. The earliest from whom descents are likely to be traced in England came here in Cromwell's time, the first public synagogue and burial ground being opened in London in 1657. Being gregarious they remained in a relatively few centres and if they had property invariably left wills. An index of all the ascertainable wills and administrations of Jews in the records of the Prerogative Court of Canterbury together with a concise biographical dictionary and a catalogue of Anglo-Jewish coats of arms was published as *Anglo-Jewish Notabilities* by the Jewish Historical Society of England in 1949. The marriage registers (1687–1837) kept at the Bevis Marks Synagogue, London, E.C.3, which usually give the parentage of both parties, have also been published as *Bevis Marks Records II* (1949) and the birth and burial registers can be seen at the Synagogue. The considerable records accumulated by the Jewish Museum at the Offices of the United Synagogue at Woburn House, Tavistock Square, London, W.1, were catalogued by C. Roth, *Archives of the United Synagogue* (1930). There is an admirable article on 'Sources of Anglo-Jewish Genealogy' by W. S. Samuel in *The Genealogists' Magazine* (Vol. VI, p. 146; supplemented at Vol. XI, p. 412) which should be consulted by all those who are interested.

It remains to mention those other religious communities which came to England as a result of economic or religious persecution abroad. Foremost among these were the Huguenots who came over in two waves about 1550 and 1680. The French Protestant Church in Soho Square received a charter in 1550 and the registers, which start in 1599, together with some 30 others for other churches in London, Norwich (from 1595), Canterbury (from 1581) and Southampton (from 1567) and elsewhere are deposited with the other Non-Parochial Registers at the Land

Registry Building. They have practically all been published by the Huguenot Society which has a large collection of Huguenot material at its Library which is at present situated at London University. This Society has also published eight volumes of denizations, naturalizations and returns of aliens, covering the period 1509–1800, which are of immense value in the tracing of foreigners of all kinds. This series is continued by *Index to Local and Personal Acts, 1801–1947* (H.M.S.O. 1949) which indexes naturalizations by Act of Parliament during that period. Following the Act of 1844 the Home Office published, in 1908, an index of the persons to whom certificates of naturalization had been granted between 1844 and 1900.

Among the Non-Parochial Registers deposited at the Land Registry Building and detailed in the above mentioned list, are several which belonged to Conforming bodies and these are perhaps worth mentioning here. They include the Registers of the Chapels Royal, Greenwich Hospital, Chelsea Hospital, Foundling Hospital, nineteenth-century cemeteries in Eccleshall, Leeds, Liverpool, and Walworth, as well as the marriage registers of Mayfair Chapel, the Mint in Southwark, the Fleet Prison, and the King's Bench Prison. These latter, which total some 300 marriage registers, all date before Lord Hardwicke's Marriage Act of 1754 and record runaway marriages solemnized without banns or licence by clergy who had ' neither liberty, money, nor credit to lose by any proceedings which the bishop could institute ', this particularly being the case where the officiating clergy were themselves in the King's Bench or Fleet Prison!

CHAPTER SIX

Filling in the Details: Education and Occupation

T HE RECORDS of schools and professions not only help to fill in the details of the personal lives of your ancestors but may very well also be the means by which you trace their ancestry as in many cases they give the parentage of the persons concerned.

School records have naturally survived rather haphazardly but many of the older Public Schools and Grammar Schools have published annotated registers of their pupils which have sometimes been compiled from general sources other than a register as such. Some of these, like J. B. Whitmore and G. R. Y. Radcliffe's *Record of Old Westminsters*, have entailed a lifetime of devoted research, and as they rarely relate to any particular area of the country it is useful to have a large collection of them together, as there is on the shelves of the Society of Genealogists, where they can be consulted one after the other. University Records form a much more consistent pattern in that the father's name and occupation is usually given. Complete lists have been published from the University registers, for Oxford *A Biographical Register of the University of Oxford to A.D. 1500* edited by A. B. Emden (3 vols., 1957–9) and *Alumni Oxonienses 1500–1886* edited by Joseph Foster (8 vols., 1887–92), and for Cambridge before 1900 *Alumni Cantabrigienses* edited by J. and J. A. Venn (10 vols., 1922–54). Many of the individual colleges have also printed and annotated their registers and these often contain much more detail than the above lists.

The other general sources of information on the education of your ancestors are apprenticeship records. In 1710 a tax was placed on apprenticeship indentures which thus came to be registered for a hundred years until the removal of the tax in 1810. The resulting records which usually give the name of the apprentice's father or guardian, the master's name and trade, and the premium and tax paid, are now at the Public Record Office. The name of the father is not usually given after 1750 when they naturally become of less value genealogically. Those covering the period 1710–74 were copied, arranged in alphabetical order, and typed by the Society of Genealogists where they are most easily consulted. There is also at the Society an index to the masters 1710–62, together with seventeen volumes of original apprenticeship indentures 1641–1888 which have been collected from various sources. The above tax did not apply to parish or public charities, the records of which may well survive in the parish chest or in the borough archives as they do at Bristol.

The lists of apprentices to the various Guilds or Companies throughout the country form with their other records another important source which covers an even greater period of time, many of the London City Company records beginning in the sixteenth century or earlier and extending to the present day. A large number of these have been deposited in the Guildhall Library and are listed in *Guide to the Records in the Corporation of London Record Office and in the Guildhall Library Muniment Room* (1950). In the provinces lists like those of the cutlers at Sheffield, of the hostmen at Newcastle upon Tyne or of the church guild at Luton may also have survived.

The records of the Services are perhaps the next most important group. Printed Lists of Army Officers have appeared annually since 1754 although there is a recently printed list for 1740, but to find details of other ranks one must know the regiment in which they served. If this is known you can then consult the Muster Books (from 1708) and the Description Books (from 1756) at the Public Record Office both of which give ages and places of birth when the soldier first appears.

The Navy List has been printed since 1749. Ships' Musters (from 1688) and Pay Books (from 1669) are at the Public Record Office, but here again you will have to know the name of the appropriate ship before you can consult them. The Lieutenants' Passing Certificates (from 1691) generally have baptismal certificates attached. The National Maritime Museum's *Commissioned Sea Officers of the Royal Navy 1660–1815* (3 vols., 1955) gives details of their careers but nothing as to place of birth or parentage.

The *Guide to the Contents of the Public Record Office* (1963) gives details of all the other service records, of which there are many classes, in the Public Record Office. The Trinity House Petitions at the Society of Genealogists contain much information on the families of merchant seamen from about 1780 to 1854.

The majority of the Clergy are found in University Registers, Crockford's *Clerical Directory* being first issued in 1858 although there are a few other earlier Clergy Lists. Records of Institutions will normally be found in the registers of the bishops of the appropriate dioceses but there are Institution Books (from 1556) at the Public Record Office. Some of the other religious denominations have also published lists of their ministers, e.g. *Ministers and Probationers of the Methodist Church* (1947) which gives a cumulative list of 9,000 ' Ministers who have died in the Work '.

For the Law the records of some of the Inns of Court have been published and these usually give the name and occupation of the father of those admitted. There are printed Law Lists from 1775, the articles of clerkship of solicitors and attorneys from 1730 being at the Public Record Office among the records of the various Courts, those of the King's Bench and Common Pleas having the greatest number.

Medical men may be found in the records of the Barber-Surgeons Company and the Society of Apothecaries which are deposited in the Guildhall Library, in the licences issued by the various bishops following the Act of 1529, in the lists of graduates in medicine at Oxford or Cambridge, or in the records of the Royal Colleges of Physicians and Surgeons. The biographies of Fellows and, up to 1825, Licentiates of the former are given in Munk's *Roll of the Royal College of Physicians of London, 1518-1925* (4 vols., 1878-1955) and of the latter in Plarr's *Lives of the Fellows of the Royal College of Surgeons* (2 vols., 1930) which was founded in 1800. The licences granted by the Bishop of London are listed in J. J. Bloom and R. R. James's *Medical Practitioners in the Diocese of London 1529-1725* (1935) but no similar lists for other dioceses have beeen published. The *Medical Register* has appeared since 1858 although there are a few earlier *Medical Directories*.

Many of the other professions have their own printed lists and biographical dictionaries; the civil service, painters and engravers, architects, musicians, judges, Members of Parliament, to mention only a few. With regard to the holders of public offices in England there is an excellent ' Bibliographical Guide to the Lists of English Office-Holders' in *Handbook of British Chronology* (Royal Historical Society, 2nd ed., 1961).

The general biographical dictionaries may also be of value for information on prominent individuals, in particular the *Dictionary of National Biography* (23 vols., 1908-13). A complete list of all peerages ever created with details of their holders is *The Complete Peerage* (13 vols., 1910–59), of Baronets is *The Complete Baronetage* (6 vols., 1900–9), and of Knights is W. A. Shaw's *Knights of England* (2 vols., 1906) although the latter is not complete for the earlier periods. All present peers and baronets with details of their ancestry and of the descendants of former holders of their titles may be found in *Burke's Peerage* (latest edition 1967). The pedigrees of untitled landed families of distinguished descent may be found in *Burke's Landed Gentry* (latest edition 1969).

Not many of us, however, are lucky enough to have had ancestors who could write, let alone keep records of their own careers, but those who left diaries which have survived are listed in *British Diaries 1442–1942* by W. Matthews (1950). This includes details as to which have been printed and the whereabouts of the originals. Like the country squire's account books, however, they mention many of the ordinary people that they came into contact with or employed and are well worth hunting for. For this reason alone it is worth getting to know the main families which held land in the particular areas in which you are interested and the present whereabouts of any of their papers. The County Record Offices will probably be able to give you information about this.

For the great number of traders and shop-keepers it is perhaps worth noting here the great series of printed Directories which have appeared in the past. County and town directories, which gave much the same sort of information as they do today, exist from the middle of the eighteenth century. The first London Directory was printed in 1677 but the regular series does not begin until 1740. All known editions are described in C. W. F.

Goss's *The London Directories 1677–1855* (1932) and those for the rest of the country in Jane E. Norton's *Guide to the National and Provincial Directories of England and Wales (excluding London) before 1856* (1950) both of which give the locations of known copies of the directories.

Other forms of directory are the poll books and voters' lists of those who held sufficient land to qualify them to vote, although these will not normally give the occupations of the persons listed except in the case of the lists of Liverymen voting in the City of London. They exist for some counties from the early eighteenth century and not only show the politics of the voter but may also indicate the movement of a family when its place of residence is different from that of the land in respect of which it is voting. The Society of Genealogists has published a list of the Poll Books in its possession (1961) and also has a typescript *Index to Voters residing in a County other than that in which their Freehold was situated* compiled from forty-one such Poll Books covering the period 1702–1807. Exact details of land ownership are often difficult to come by and although registries of deeds were established in the reign of Queen Anne for Middlesex and Yorkshire, a general system of land registration did not come into operation until very recent times. Because of this it is perhaps worth mentioning the official *Return of Owners of Land* published in 1873–6 which has alphabetical lists for each county of the British Isles. It forms a valuable directory of the country at that time and is now of sufficient antiquity to be of interest to the genealogist, being called by them the ' Modern Domesday Book '. If you have dreams of unclaimed acres or family estates that is the book to dispel them!

CHAPTER SEVEN

The Public Record Office and the British Museum Library

THE PUBLIC RECORD OFFICE, known to historians generally as the P.R.O., was built in 1856 to house the records accumulated by the various departments of State and the more important secular courts, at that time dispersed between the Tower of London, the Rolls Chapel, and elsewhere. Generally records over fifty years old and nearly all over a hundred years old are available for public examination free of charge provided a Reader's Ticket is held. This latter can be obtained by applying to the Keeper of the Records, Public Record Office, Chancery Lane, London. There are now some forty-seven miles of shelving here and at Ashridge (used to store less-used records) and a further 114 miles at two other intermediate repositories.

Some of the classes of records at the office which are consulted by genealogists we have already mentioned, the Census Returns (p. 17), the Non-parochial Registers (p. 33), the Apprenticeship Indentures (p. 37), and the Army and Navy Records (p. 38) in particular, but as can be seen from the two volumes of the *Guide to the Contents of the Public Record Office* (1963) there are many others which are of considerable value from all historical points of view. The first two classes of record mentioned above are now housed by the P.R.O. at the Land Registry Building.

Many of the classes of documents of which I will try to give some indication are in Latin which was the language of most official documents up to the Restoration (1660) and was not finally abolished as such until 1731. Because of this and the difficulties of the handwriting of these documents it may well be worth employing a professional searcher. The Public Record Office has a list of such searchers, or you can use that supplied by the Society of Genealogists.

We usually do not like the idea of our ancestors having had collisions with the law even as witnesses at somebody else's trial but one of the most valuable sources of genealogical information is the records of the English courts of law and, in particular, of the Court of Chancery. It is the depositions (i.e., statements of evidence) of the witnesses which are most useful, but as the suits are only indexed under the plaintiff's surname and there is no indication of the county concerned after 1714 (except as regards the index of places mentioned in the calendar of the Rolls of Decrees), they are obviously of little practical value unless your ancestor was a plaintiff or was known to have been concerned with a particular case. They are in the Long Room at the P.R.O. An index to a very large number of the deponents in the suits was fortunately compiled by the late C. A. Bernau and a microfilm of this has recently been acquired by the Society of Genealogists (the original having gone to America); when this is available it will be the most convenient means of consulting the Chancery Depositions.

The depositions in the Court of Exchequer form a similarly valuable series, and have better indexes, the indexes of cases being arranged by county and Mr. Bernau's index just mentioned covering all the depositions taken in the country by commission (1559–1800).

For those families which held land directly from the King the series of Inquisitions post mortem are particularly valuable, being inquests taken upon the death of any supposed tenant in chief, particularizing the lands of the deceased, giving the date of his death and the name, age and relationship of his next heir. There are duplicate series in the Chancery Records and in those of the Exchequer, and, after 1540, a further copy was sent to the Court of Wards and Liveries. They extend in date from the reign of Henry III to that of Charles II and the P.R.O. is printing indexes which have so far covered the period from Henry III to 1377 and from 1485 to 1509. The Index Library and other societies have printed partial indexes relating to some particular counties, e.g. Devon and Cornwall 1216–1649 and London 1484–1603.

Of the other records in the P.R.O. (and even to a certain

extent the above) the beginner usually has considerable difficulty in understanding not only the documents themselves but the indexes and calendars, and this is not only due to the peculiarities of the handwriting and the shortened forms of Latin words so loved by the legal clerks but also to the terminology and arrangement of the records. For these reasons I would not advise anyone who has not already had some considerable experience in tackling the above classes of records to attempt to find their way around the following. In any case, a look at what few printed calendars there are will probably put you off consulting the originals despite the amount of information they contain.

Feet of Fines are the duplicate copies of agreements relating to land which were retained by the king's justices and result from usually fictitious actions being brought by the purchasers so as to get the agreement registered. The extraordinary name they have comes from the fact that they were the 'final' end of the dispute, the copy held by the justice being called a 'pes' and mistranslated into 'foot', it being the old French for 'peace'. They run from 1190 to 1833 and are amongst the records of the Court of Common Pleas.

The lack of a general system of land registration led in the same way to the enrolling of deeds and conveyances between private persons on the back of the Close Rolls, so called because the face was used to enroll private instructions to officers of the Crown and others. Thus enrolled are settlements, quitclaims, deeds of bargain and sale and of lease and release, surrenders of offices, disentailing assurances, deeds poll of change of name, deeds and wills of Papists, etc. They have been printed to 1500 by the P.R.O.

The Patent Rolls contain the enrolments of royal grants of lands, liberties and privileges to corporations and to individuals, presentations to Crown livings and appointments to offices of various kinds. Many of the denizations mentioned in Chapter Five are taken from these Rolls. Indexes down to 1566 have been printed by the P.R.O. The Charter Rolls which contained much the same sort of information have all been printed down to 1516 when the series ends.

Subsidy Rolls, which are fortunately arranged topographically, contain, up to the reign of Charles II, the names of all persons assessed towards the payment of the aids, subsidies, and other contributions granted to the Crown by Parliament or by the Clergy in Convocation and thus subdivided into two series, 'Lay' and 'Clerical'. One of the better known of these is the Hearth Tax of 1660-74 which includes exemption certificates for those too poor to pay the tax. Together with the series is another of Certificates of Residence relating to those who were assessed in one place but who had meanwhile moved to another, thus being valuable evidence of removals.

A list of a different nature is that of all persons holding offices, including the Freemen of all the London Companies and the clergy and gentry of England and Wales, who signed the Association Oath Rolls of William III (1696). (These latter may be likened to the Protestation Oath Rolls of 1641–2 at the House of Lords Record Office described in the Fifth Report of the Royal Commission on Historical Manuscripts (1876) which lists the parishes for which returns have survived).

At the P.R.O. itself there is a *Catalogue of Lists and Indexes* which indicates under every class of record all the means of reference thereto. The published indexes and calendars of records issued in general collections or in series by public bodies (including the P.R.O.) or private societies are all analytically described in *Texts and Calendars* by E. L. C. Mullins (Royal Historical Society, 1958) and similar odd volumes of indexes issued by private persons and generally relating to one county only are listed in *A Select Bibliography of English Genealogy* by H. G. Harrison (1937) both being supplemented by the *Handlist of Record Publications* (1951) and the *Handlist of Scottish and Welsh Record Publications* (1954) published by the British Records Association.

The Search Rooms of the P.R.O. are open from 9.30 a.m. to 5 p.m. from Monday to Friday, and from 9.30 a.m. to 1 p.m. on Saturday. It is closed during the week ending with the last Saturday in September. I should, perhaps, point out that applications for documents should be in by 3.30 p.m.; applications for those required on a Saturday must be received not later than midday on the preceding day. All documents have to be applied for by filling in a form with the appropriate reference number, which the attendants will always help you to find, and there is a delay of up to an hour before they are produced. The Land Registry Building is unfortunately not open on Saturday mornings.

The British Museum Library is Britain's largest repository of all being arranged in one chronological sequence and bound 'Copyright Libraries' (the Bodleian at Oxford, Cambridge University Library, the National Library of Wales, the Scottish National Library, and Trinity College at Dublin) a copy of every book published, these being added to the large collections of books already held and in particular to the Royal Library (given in 1757 which had had the right of claiming a copy of any book registered at Stationers' Hall and, since 1814, of any book published). The catalogue of these, by the author, is in the Reading Room there, and, having been printed, may be seen together with the volumes of the Subject Index in many large Public Libraries. I am not going to dwell further on the collection of printed books except in one particular instance because most people with the help of their Public Libraries and the inter-library loan system (of which even the Society of Genealogists is a member), can obtain almost any work required with little difficulty and should thus regard the British Museum as a place of last resort.

One section of the Department of Printed Books, however, which is of particular genealogical interest is the collection of newspapers of which in the case of many series there are no other copies. Those before 1800 are at the British Museum and catalogued under 'Periodical Publications' in the General Catalogue. Those from 1801 onwards are at the British Museum Newspaper Library, Colindale, London, N.W.9. There is a printed catalogue of the provincial newspapers and another of all those relating to the nineteenth century. *The Tercentenary Handlist of English and Welsh Newspapers* published by *The Times* in 1920 is a list of all formerly and then existing newspapers arranged chronologically, whereas G. A. Cranfield's *Hand-List of English Provincial Newspapers and Periodicals 1700–1760* is arranged geographically. This latter list gives locations of other sets of the papers apart from those in the British Museum and there is a useful list of 'Newspapers on Microfilm' with locations of copies in Volume 62, p. 256, of the *Library Association Record* (1960).

Most of the early newspapers in the British Museum are in Dr. Charles Burney's Collection which begins in 1619 and is par-ticularly valuable for the eighteenth century. His Collection con-tains Irish papers from 1691, Scottish from 1708, English provincial from 1712 and even a large number of American papers, all being arranged in one chronological sequence and bound together in volumes. *The Times* is the only newspaper which has published an index from early times and although this does not include the births, deaths, and marriages, *Palmer's Index to The Times* (published quarterly since 1791) is invaluable for tracing those other events in one's life, or in one's ancestors' lives, which are reported in 'the press'. In this connection it is perhaps worth mentioning here that *The Gentleman's Magazine* which appeared from 1731 to 1868 contains a very large number of death and marriage notices. Besides the annual indexes there are consolidated indexes of all names mentioned (by surname only) in two volumes covering the period 1731–1818, and fuller indexes of obituaries and marriages have been published more recently, i.e., *An Index to the Biographical and Obituary Notices in the Gentleman's Magazine 1731–80* (1891) and E. A. Fry's *An Index to the Marriages in the Gentleman's Magazine 1731–1768*. Sir William Musgrave's *Obituary prior to 1800*, published as volumes 44–9 of the Harleian Society series, forms an invaluable index to notices of deaths which appeared in similar magazines like the *Historical Register* and *Annual Register*. The use of newspapers to the genealogist is amply illustrated in *The Genealogical Value of the Early English Newspapers* by C. D. P. Nicholson (1934).

It is the Department of (Western) Manuscripts which offers the most, in the way of original material, to the genealogist. Catalogues of the collections which formed the nucleus of the Department, the Harleian (formed by Robert Harley, later Earl of Oxford), the Cottonian (by Sir Robert Cotton), and the Sloane (by Sir Hans Sloane), were published long ago with those of many of the other special collections, and catalogues of the 'Additional MSS' added since then have appeared over the years together with others of the great collection of Charters.

The Harleian Manuscripts are of particular interest in that they contain copies of many of the pedigrees taken at heraldic visitations (see p. 61) – which have been extended and enlarged by antiquaries and other interested persons whose hands they passed through, e.g. arms-painters and monumental masons – as well as some original visitation books and papers from the collections of Heralds, such as Anstis, Dugdale, Lee, Le Neve, and Segar. Of the collections of historians relating to particular counties, Cole's Cambridgeshire, Burrell's Sussex, Wolley's Derbyshire, Jermyn and Davy's Suffolk, may be mentioned along with Gerish's copies of the monumental inscriptions in Hertfordshire and Buckler's topographical drawings. Some of the largest collections are those of private and state papers of men like Burghley, Harley, Newcastle, Hardwicke, Canning, Liverpool, Lauderdale, Aberdeen, Peel, Nelson, General Gordon, Wellesley, Warren Hastings, and Gladstone, all rich in biographical material.

Along the side of the Manuscripts Room are the many volumes of the classified subject index to the manuscripts. Five volumes of this are entitled 'Biography – Notes and Genealogies' and the other subject headings of interest are 'Heraldry', 'Topography', and 'Private Letters'. There is a simple reference system, applications for manuscripts being made on printed forms, and production following in less than an hour.

The collections housed in the British Museum Library are outlined in Arundell Esdaile's *The British Museum Library* (1946) which gives details of all the published catalogues. Entrance to the Reading Room and the Department of Manuscripts is by ticket only and applications for these should be made in writing to the Director stating the purpose of the enquiry and enclosing a letter of recommendation from someone in a recognized position. The ticket for the Reading Room will also admit you to the Newspaper Library at Colindale but a separate ticket is required for the Department of Manuscripts. They are not issued to anyone under twenty-one. The Reading Room is open all day Saturday and until 9 p.m. on Tuesdays, Wednesdays and Thursdays and it is possible to put in applications for books on Saturdays and after normal working hours on the other three days. This is a considerable help to those who cannot use the library at other times.

CHAPTER EIGHT

The Society of Genealogists

T HE S OCIETY OF G ENEALOGISTS is composed of a collection of people throughout the world interested in genealogy, topography, and heraldry, who pay an annual subscription to support the organization of a library, magazine. and genealogical service for their benefit and the promotion of interest in genealogy generally, being an ' association not for profit '.

It was founded in 1911 and is now situated in a very fine Victorian house at 37 Harrington Gardens, London, S.W.7, near to Gloucester Road Underground Station. Membership is open to anyone who can give suitable references or the recommendations of two persons who are already members, the entrance fee being one and a half guineas. The annual subscription for Town Members (i.e. those residing within twenty-five miles of Trafalgar Square) is four guineas, and for Country and Overseas Members, three guineas. Students are admitted at half the usual entrance fee and annual subscription. The above subscriptions include a quarterly *Genealogists' Magazine,* the official journal of the Society. Meetings are arranged during the winter months and these are open to non-members.

Members have access to the Library of nearly 30,000 books, the manuscript collection, and the card indexes, nearly all of which are on open shelves so that they can browse to their hearts' content. They may also borrow printed books from the library with certain exceptions. The rooms are open also to the searches of non-members on payment of search fees, 15s. for half a day, 22s. 6d. for a whole day, and 30s. for a day and evening, during the usual hours 10 – 6 Tuesdays and Fridays, 10 – 9 Wednesdays and Thursdays, and 10 – 5 Saturdays. The Library is closed on Mondays.

I have already made frequent mention to special features of the Society's library which is unique in this country. A very short guide is available for beginners and my article *Collections and Indexes of the Society of Genealogists* in Volume 13, p. 311, of the *Genealogists' Magazine* gives further details. This latter was reprinted in the *Genealogists' Handbook* edited by Peter Spufford and myself for the Society in 1969. All the books which relate directly to any particular county are placed together, local record society transactions, county histories, parish histories, parish registers, directories, monumental inscriptions and poll books, in alphabetical order of county. The printed catalogue of the Society's collection of parish registers, the largest in the country, is mentioned on page 24. Many of the copies end in 1812 and very few are carried beyond 1837 when General Registration started.

The remainder of the library is divided into the following sections:

(a) THE SERVICES; Army, Navy and Airforce Lists, regimental histories, naval biographical dictionaries.

(b) RELIGIONS; publications of Catholic Record Society, Huguenot Society, Society of Friends, Clergy Lists, nonconformist material.

(c) TRADES AND PROFESSIONS; Law Lists, Medical Registers, biographical dictionaries of particular professions, e.g. architects and painters, firm histories, lists of members of professional bodies.

(d) PUBLIC RECORDS; calendars of some of the most useful from the genealogical point of view.

(e) BIOGRAPHY; Dictionary of National Biography, some of the older biographical dictionaries.

(f) PERIODICALS; Index Library, Harleian Society volumes, Camden Society, genealogical periodicals, e.g. *The Ancestor, The Genealogist, Miscellanea Genealogica et Heraldica, The Pedigree Register, Notes and Queries, The Gentleman's Magazine* and similar magazines, Historical Manuscripts Commission Reports.

(g) DIRECTORIES; covering more than one county arranged in chronological order.

(h) TEXTBOOKS; guides to genealogical research and repositories, gazetteers, dictionaries of surnames, lists of parish registers, parish maps, lists of printed pedigrees and family histories.

(i) SCHOOLS AND UNIVERSITIES; lists of entrants to schools and universities and their histories, records of the Inns of Court.

(j) SCOTLAND; formed mainly of periodical publications and local histories, including Scottish Record Society indexes of Wills.

(k) WALES; a small section.

(l) IRELAND; including a series of Dublin Directories, abstracts of destroyed Irish wills, manuscript lists, local history, published calendars of Wills and Marriage Licences.

(m) PEERAGE; all the early peerages, long runs of Burke and Debrett and the *Landed Gentry*, Walford, Kelly, *Who's Who*, *Complete Peerage*, *Complete Baronetage*, Knightages, Royal Descents.

(n) WILLS AND MARRIAGE LICENCES; all calendars published privately and some manuscript indexes and abstracts.

(o) HERALDRY; standard textbooks, Burke's *Armory*, Papworth's *Ordinary*, Fairbairn's *Crests*, collection of Armorial Illustrations arranged by family.

(p) AMERICA; mainly works on emigrants and publications of genealogical societies.

(q) COMMONWEALTH AND FORMER POSSESSIONS; large index of English people in India, early colonial directories, lists of settlers.

(r) FOREIGN; small sections from most countries, mainly Peerage, English settlement registers and monumental inscriptions.

This rough list, of course, is far from complete in detail but it should give some idea of the sources available.

All the printed family histories, including a very large number of privately printed ones are kept in alphabetical order together with those manuscript and typescript histories which have been bound, some of which run to many volumes. The printed family histories are included in T. R. Thomson's *Catalogue of British Family Histories* (1935) but the other two lists mentioned on page 11 should also be consulted, remembering, of course, that these only cover *printed* material.

Loose pedigrees, will abstracts and probate copies, original deeds, letters, copies of monumental inscriptions, marriage licences, grants of arms, rough notes, and anything else of genealogical value are all filed in foolscap envelopes in alphabetical order of surname in box files. Those documents which relate to several families in some particular place are filed by parish under County, the two series together filling nearly a thousand box files. This collection has been formed mainly from the donations and bequests of members, although much of the original material received in recent years has come from the British Records Association. A large number of roll-pedigrees stored separately are indexed in the 'Family History' section of the library catalogue.

The Society's Great Card Index of some three million references is arranged under surname, and subdivided by christian name, and forms an excellent guide to the distribution of any given surname, being composed of all sorts of genealogical information taken from a variety of sources and indexing many complete parish registers, general genealogical works, marriage licences, monumental inscriptions, and Chancery Proceedings. There are several smaller indexes, including one similar to the Great Card Index but arranged by county and parish, Harvey Bloom's Index of Stray Wills, Glencross's Cornish Index, the Fawcett Index of Clergy and North Country families, Whitfield's Shropshire Index, and the index to the thousands of deeds which passed through the hands of the dealer James Coleman, as well as several indexes and manuscript collections relating to particular families on which an unusually large amount of work has been done (e.g. Bateman, Willis, Pemberton, Berney, Finny, Scattergood, Carden, Mann).

Boyd's Marriage Index is perhaps the most well known of the Society's genealogical tools. Compiled by the late Percival Boyd between 1925 and 1955 from the parish registers, Bishops' transcripts, and marriage licences of the country, it is limited to the period 1538–1837. The Index at present fills some 531 volumes and covers almost 3,000 parishes, having about six to seven million names. It is arranged by county in periods of twenty-five years and has separate volumes in each of these periods for sixteen different counties (Cambridgeshire, Cornwall, Cumberland, Derbyshire, Devon, Durham, Essex, Gloucestershire, Lancashire, London and Middlesex, Norfolk, Northumberland, Shropshire, Somerset, Suffolk, Yorkshire), none of them entirely complete, these again often being subdivided into men and women. A mass of marriages from the other counties and other sources like the *Gentleman's Magazine* were indexed into two miscellaneous series, divided into similar periods and sections. The whole is described in *A Key to Boyd's Marriage Index* (completely revised by myself in 1963) which lists all the parishes and periods covered except those in the Miscellaneous sections and describes the system of abbreviation used. Copies of certain parts of the index are to be found in various libraries and a card index of all the marriages in Hertfordshire (1538–1837) is at Hertford Record Office. No similar index exists anywhere for baptisms and burials, although a scheme is now being actively considered, but there is an incomplete index of burials in the London area, also compiled by the indefatigable Mr. Boyd, in sixteen volumes and covering the period 1538-1853, also at the Society.

Another of Mr. Boyd's great works is known as the *Inhabitants of London* and attempts to 'gather together on one sheet, in addition to the dates of birth and death, residence and company of any given citizen, the names of his parents, his marriage or marriages and his children with their marriages, and a reference to his will'. The collection is particularly valuable for families in the sixteenth and seventeenth centuries although it does cover a wider period. There are 238 volumes containing details of 59,389 persons and a collective index.

The Apprentices of Great Britain covering the period 1710–74 and the collection of original apprenticeship indentures are described on page 37.

The largest collection of original documents are the Trinity House Petitions bound in alphabetical order in 102 volumes and consisting of petitions from seafaring men (mostly of the Mercantile Marine) and their dependants for assistance from the Corporation of Trinity House between 1780 and 1854. Many of the applicants enclosed supporting documents and original certificates which make the collection of great genealogical and biographical value.

Apart from the local collections mentioned above, the Snell Collection contains abstracts of many Berkshire Wills, the Campling Collection much Norfolk and Suffolk material, that of F. C. Beazley some for Cheshire, Mrs. Smith a great deal for the West Indies, Welply for abstracts of the destroyed Irish Wills, and the great Macleod Collection in 279 folders for Scottish families.

The Society has a small staff which undertakes research for members and non-members both in its own rooms and elsewhere and details of the scale of charges can be obtained from the Director of Research. The Society can also furnish a list of professional record searchers who have been recommended by two of its members, and the Public Record Office and most County Record Offices have similar lists. It is hardly necessary to say that you should agree your terms before the work is undertaken or set a limit to the expense to be incurred. It is practically impossible to estimate the cost of tracing a pedigree as any reader of this book will see, so the Society usually works on a daily basis although it will undertake specific searches of particular records calculated hourly as will most record searchers.

There is no organization which registers the qualifications of professional genealogists or regulates their fees and any person may set up as a genealogist without any previous experience whatsoever and charge whatever he chooses. For this reason alone it is worth taking the precautions mentioned, or, better still, doing the work yourself and only employing a professional when some special difficulty arises. If you do employ a professional I would strongly suggest that you employ a member of the Association of Genealogists and Record Agents which was formed in 1968 to help remedy the above-mentioned position.

CHAPTER NINE

County, Municipal, and Diocesan Record Offices

THE DIVISION of England into counties and their administration by Justices of the Peace and County Councils forms
a series of records around which have grown up the County
Record Offices now to be found in most county-towns. Similarly
the records of city and ecclesiastical administration form the
nuclei of municipal and diocesan record offices.

County Record Offices are administered by County Councils
through their County Archivists and are open much in the same
way as Public Reference Libraries although, owing to shortage of
space, some require an appointment in advance. They are all
listed, together with their full addresses and hours of opening in
the British Records Association's *List of Record Repositories in
Great Britain* (1968). This list also indicates which repositories
are able to furnish copies of documents for students and for which
Guides are known to exist – either printed or duplicated – to the
whole or part of their collections.

Before the passing of the Local Government Act in 1888 the
Justices of the Peace were the main administrators in our English
counties and their records, the Quarter Sessions Records,
naturally form one of the most important series in County Record
Office accumulations, usually being extant at least from the mid-
seventeenth century onwards. They contain along with other
officially deposited records much that is of value to the genealogist, settlement orders for vagrants, bastardy maintenance orders,
licences for inns and religious meeting houses, jury panels, sacra-
ment certificates and oaths of allegiance, registers of Papists'
estates, lists of badgers, entries of gamekeepers and certificates

55

for killing game, as well as the usual indictments, recognizances and petitions, all giving the places of abode and occupation of those mentioned. A few have been printed, Hertfordshire even as far as 1843, and a bibliography appears in F. G. Emmison and Irvine Gray's *County Records* (2nd ed., 1963).

The Enclosure Awards of Fields and Commons in the eighteenth and nineteenth centuries form another valuable source. They are usually accompanied by good maps with long schedules of owners and occupiers showing the distribution of the land in the parish and enabling one to identify the present position of formerly held properties. Two copies were made and both have usually survived, one in the custody of the parish and the other in the County Record Office. Their dates are usually given in the parish articles in the Victoria County History and there is a bibliography of county lists in *Village Records* by John West (1962).

Land Tax Assessments for each parish are usually filed with the Quarter Sessions Records and give the names of landowners, the occupiers of their land, their rateable value, and the amount assessed. The system started in 1692 and *County Records* gives a list of the dates from which records have survived in each county. Similarly lists of Freeholders, Jurors, and Electors, usually give the occupations and more recently the exact abode of those eligible to vote or voting. In this class fall also the printed Poll Books which many Record Offices have made a point of collecting.

Like Enclosure Awards the Tithe Awards made between 1836 and 1860 give schedules of owners and occupiers with detailed maps and exist for most parishes in triplicate at the Public Record Office, in the Diocesan Record Office and in the hands of the Incumbent. *Village Records* gives a partial bibliography by county of these interesting documents with photographs and long extracts from a Worcestershire example.

With regard to parish and county maps some Record Offices have taken considerable interest in collecting maps of their counties at particular periods as well as other parish and estate maps and maps relating to turnpikes, canal and railway development, as well as those drawn up as a result of schemes for lighting, paving and sewage, most of which give detailed lists of the occupants of the sites to be affected. Again *Village Records* has a useful county bibliography.

The special provision taken for the care, restoration and storage of documents in County Record Offices has led many private individuals to deposit in them estate and family archives and more recently the older firms of solicitors have found this a convenient means of clearing their strongrooms. Their records are naturally more concerned with the conveyancing of land and its descent. Thus whole series of manor court records have been deposited by some families with large estates in those offices which have been approved by the Master of the Rolls for the reception of Manorial material. The loose deeds acquired in this way are usually the subject of some form of card index compiled by the Office and include conveyances, leases, mortgages, marriage settlements, m inorial surrenders and admissions, and probate copies of wills. Privately deposited collections contain a wide range of other material, private letters, household accounts, diaries etc., some of which cover many generations and many of which have a more than local importance. Diocesan Record Offices had long been used by Bishops for the deposit of their records but in 1929 the Parochial Records Measure allowed them to appoint repositories for the receipt of parochial documents found in unsafe custody. Some extended their own offices or nominated the County Record Offices or large reference libraries like Birmingham for this purpose. As a result the main series of ecclesiastical records, Act and Visitation Books, Bishops' Transcripts of Parish Registers, Bonds and Allegations for Marriage Licences and Wills have become accessible to students. Following the compulsory deposit of those parochial records found in unsafe conditions many Record Offices have taken active steps to persuade the clergy to deposit their Parish Registers, Churchwardens' Accounts, Poor Rate Books, Settlement Papers and those other records to be found in their Parish Chests. In some cases fees are charged for the consultation of ecclesiastical records but this practice varies from diocese to diocese. As a result of this activity most of the London Parish Registers have been deposited in the Guildhall Library, many for Wales in the National Library of Wales at Aberystwyth, nearly all those for Berkshire in the Record Office at Reading, and over a third of those for Warwickshire in the Record Office in the county town, to mention only a few.

The staff of County Record Offices and most other archive

repositories is generally small and cannot be expected to make lengthy searches but they can usually give the name of a locally resident professional searcher who is familiar with the records of the County. A few have published very full guides to their material (e.g. Kent, Lancashire, Berkshire, Essex) and most have some form of outline list of their major collections.

Many of the larger public libraries have local history collections which should certainly not be neglected. In many of the larger towns the borough records are to be found in the Public Library (e.g. Manchester, Harrogate); some have estate and family collections and those of local societies, and some the records of local business houses and schools. A useful article on those libraries which have manuscript collections is ' Archives and Manuscripts in Libraries ' in Volume 64, p. 269, of *Library Association Record* (1962).

CHAPTER TEN

Heraldic Ancestors

THE ORIGIN of heraldry is something which fortunately does not concern us here. It is a much disputed subject. Suffice it to say that by the end of the twelfth century persons of the knightly class were using lance flags and shields painted with easily distinguishable patterns and devices as a form of personal mark which could clearly be seen in battle and recognized at tournaments. This pattern or heraldic device was also used on seals where it first appears as part of a picture of the 'signatory'. Representing as it did the feudal symbol by which the men recognized their lord, it passed as a symbol to the lord's sons and their descendants being altered or 'differenced' according to their relationship but retaining the main features of the old heraldic device so that anyone using a 'differenced' device could be presumed to descend from the original user, thus making heraldry a subject of considerable interest to the genealogist.

It is from the depiction of the shield on seals that the present forms of representation descend. The shield soon became the sole or principal device on the seal. Then when some shape or 'crest' came to be worn on top of the helmet, this was also shown on the seal above the shield. On a circular seal this left space which was filled with the decorative flowing 'mantling' which was the cloth draped over the helmet to keep the sun off, cut through of course by many sword thrusts and kept in place by a 'crest wreath'. On the great seals of the barons any further space was filled with representations of animals, birds, or mythical beasts, which were usually shown as supporting the shield. Such 'supporters' came in this way to be regarded as one of the privileges of peers, although they are now granted to certain

Knights, to the chiefs of Scottish clans, and to certain other very privileged persons.

The reasons why certain people took certain designs is, on the whole, a mystery. It is easy to see that a raven is a reasonable choice for a man called Corbet, while cups suit the name Butler, and in Cheshire a knight may reasonably use some combination of wheat sheafs borrowed from the arms of his lord the Earl of Chester but most stories purporting to give the reason for the use of a particular coat are just as likely as Kipling's story of how the leopard got its spots or the tiger its stripes. Obviously some unrelated people ended up with the same arms and, never having disputed their rights with each other, their descendants bear those same arms to this day. Where disputes did arise they were tried before the Earl Marshal and his Court of Chivalry, a court which sat last in 1734 but was revived in 1953 when Manchester Corporation successfully brought an action against the Manchester Palace of Varieties for using the Corporation arms on the pelmet above the stage.

In the period when tournaments became so popular, the Age of Chivalry, a class of attendants was employed who could recognize the contestants from their arms and, later, being engaged generally by Lords and Kings as go-betweens in war, became known as 'Heralds' and 'Kings of Arms'. With the growing use and complexity of arms some system of registration had to be evolved and the heralds began by recording them on Rolls. In 1415 the King instituted the office of Garter King of Arms and very shortly afterwards the latter is found granting arms to new applicants and confirming arms already in use. In 1530 the two other Kings of Arms, Norroy and Clarenceux, or their deputies, were empowered to make general tours of their provinces, Norroy north of the Trent and Clarenceux south of that river, to record the arms and pedigrees of the various families entitled to arms and to remove those used without authorization. This they did at regular intervals down to the year 1687. These ' visitations ' created a vast mass of genealogical information which has almost turned the heralds into genealogists, their ceremonial functions having declined considerably over the years.

One or two of the Elizabethan heralds were not too particular about the reliability of the pedigrees they registered and this coupled with the fact that many printed visitation pedigrees were taken from the none too accurate versions in the British Museum, have given the visitations rather a bad name, something which was increased by the rivalry among the heralds themselves. The latter had been formed into a College of Arms by a charter of incorporation in 1484. The present College, which is in Queen Victoria Street, London, E.C.4, consists of three Kings of Arms (Garter, Clarenceux, Norroy and Ulster), six Heralds (Somerset, Chester, Windsor, Richmond, Lancaster, York), and four Pursuivants (Rouge Croix, Rouge Dragon, Portcullis, Bluemantle) who are all members of the Royal Household. Presiding over them all is the Hereditary Earl Marshal, the Duke of Norfolk, by whom they are nominated and by whose warrant they may grant arms. However, they hold office by Letters Patent under the Great Seal. The officers receive no salary and thus fees for information and the granting of arms are heavier here than they are in Scotland or Eire where the comparable officers receive state salaries. The records of the College are not open in any way to the public and the individual heralds have their own private 'practices' in genealogical research taking it in turns to be in waiting for the receipt of letters and callers, the hours being from 10 a.m. to 4 p.m. from Monday to Friday.

The vast genealogical and heraldic library of the College is described in A. R. Wagner's *Records and Collections of the College of Arms* (1952), the three main manuscript groups being the official visitation records, the records of grants and confirmation of arms, and the registered pedigrees, the last two groups being still in progress.

Visitations

The visitations between 1530 and 1687 conferred full rights to bear the arms therein specified on the families then recorded, the information collected being in most cases legally demonstrable although, of course, not necessarily complete. The pedigrees thus drawn up are legal evidence of a descent, provided they can be shown to be the product of a proper visitation commission, that the book in which the pedigree is contained was drawn up at that visitation, and that the book remains in the hands of its proper custodian the College of Arms. The information obtained would normally have come from the personal knowledge of the head of the family who would usually sign the finished pedigree, from his family traditions and muniments, or from the records of an earlier visitation or a pedigree drawn up in Tudor or early Stuart times. As we have seen in Chapter Seven, copies of many of the visitation pedigrees found their way into private possession and eventually into public repositories like the British Museum Library and finally were printed by private persons and societies like the Harleian Society, being 'corrected', amended, extended, and 'improved', from dubious and often unspecified sources on the way. A list of the officially recognized visitations appears in an appendix to the above mentioned Sir Anthony Wagner's *Records and Collections of the College of Arms* and this can be compared with E. N. Geijer's bibliography of printed visitations in volume 6 of *The Genealogists' Magazine*. In volume 13 of the latter magazine G. D. Squibb examines each of these printed visitations in turn, commenting on their reliability in comparison with the official records – an expert's evaluation of considerable importance.

Grants of Arms

Grants of Arms may be made to suitable applicants by the appropriate Offices of Arms. The College of Arms has jurisdiction over all persons domiciled in England, Wales, Northern Ireland, and the British Dominions and Colonies, as well as the power to register the arms of foreigners who become naturalized British subjects and to make 'honorary' grants to citizens of the United States of America. The Court of the Lord Lyon, General Register House, Edinburgh, has jurisdiction in Scotland and over cadets of Scottish families living abroad who wish to matriculate according to the laws of their ancestors. The Genealogical Office, Dublin Castle, under the Chief Herald of Ireland, has jurisdiction in Eire and may confirm by Letters Patent arms which have been used by a family for at least a hundred years and three generations, a right which Norroy and Ulster King of Arms also exercises with regard to Northern Ireland.

A 'suitable applicant' for a grant is something which has not recently been defined with any authority. Any commoner can petition for a Grant of Arms and it does not appear that any applicant is ever refused so long as the fees are paid. The fees for a Grant in England are now £157 10s. 0d. The grant is usually made to the petitioner and his descendants although it may specify also (for a further fee) the descendants of the petitioner's father or grandfather. For this fee you receive the beautifully painted Letters Patent showing the arms granted, signed and sealed by the appropriate heralds. The arms can then be used in any way desired ' according to the law of arms ' by the grantee and his descendants *in the male line only* provided that they register their descent from the grantee at the College. These latter conditions apply to any person who uses arms; he must be descended in the male line from the original grantee and he must have registered this descent at the College. If he quarters the arms of an extinct family which he represents through the marriage of one of his ancestors with the heiress, the right of that family to those arms must be shown and registered. A Grant consists of a shield and a crest, for although you can have a shield without a crest, you cannot have a crest without a shield. As we have seen supporters are only granted to certain privileged persons. The mantling and the wreath on which the crest stands are automatically made up from the chief colour and the chief metal (gold or silver) of the shield unless there are other special livery colours. Mottoes do not form a part of the Grant except in Scotland, although they may be shown in the margin of the Letters Patent; consequently they may be changed or assumed at the will of the grantee or his descendants. The position and decoration of the helmet varies according to the rank of the holder as does the coronet which any peer bears on top of the shield and under the helmet. More recently many Badges have also been granted in England, the fees for these being £62 10s. 0d. if they are included in the Grant of Arms or £68 15s. 0d. if they are made the subject of a separate grant.

There is no official printed list of the persons to whom arms have been granted in the past and no herald seems willing to say how complete are the three volumes of Grantees of Arms before 1898 published by the Harleian Society (vols. 66–8), and the Miscellaneous Grants (vols. 76–7). For Scotland, however, Sir James Balfour Paul published in 1903 *An Ordinary of Arms in the Lyon Register*, which covers the period 1672–1901. The Registers of Grants of Arms in Ireland exist from the time of Edward VI and are listed, together with recorded pedigrees, in William Skey's *Heraldic Calendar* (1846).

Registered Pedigrees

The third group of manuscript material at the College is the registered pedigrees. The immense amount of genealogical activity at the College over the years has led to an ever growing series of pedigrees, many registered at the time of granting of Arms and kept up to date by the grantees' descendants. No list of them, however, has ever been made public, although searches among them will be made and certified extracts given for certain fees.

In Ireland, and to a lesser extent in England, there exists a series of funeral certificates resulting from the display of arms at funerals which were certified by the heralds. This was particularly common in the Tudor period and degrees of pomp came to be laid down according to the rank of the deceased. They cease about 1690 when the modern undertaker or upholder took over the arrangement of funerals. The display of arms at funerals continued, however, in the form of diamond hatchments which were later hung in the church, a custom which has not entirely died out.

As will be seen from the above, the legal use of a Coat of Arms depends on one or two fairly well defined conditions. However the use of arms by unauthorized persons is only too common, particularly the arms of families of the same surname which have been taken from one of the armories, or lists of arms arranged by surname, of which the most well known is Burke's *General Armory* (1884, reprinted 1962). This illegal use of other people's arms is not a new thing and this complicates matters in that a family may have an early Victorian seal, for instance, 'which belonged to great-grandfather' which may be authentic or may just as easily be the result of those stationers' advertisements 'Send Name and County, and in Three Days you will receive a Correct Copy of your Armorial Bearings, Plain Sketch, 3s.' which were so common at the beginning of the last century. However, if used earlier than about 1820, or if the ancestor is called an Esquire, the possibility that he was really 'armigerous' and had registered arms should certainly be investigated.

The identification of a coat-of-arms or crest on a piece of 'family' silver (or indeed on that seal) is a problem which is often posed and is similar to the quartering by an ancestor of some unknown arms, both perhaps providing a valuable link with another armigerous family. The main tool here is Papworth's *Ordinary of British Armorials* (1874, reprinted 1961). The heraldic description of a coat of arms proceeds along a certain pattern which enables any coat of arms to be reduced to a written formula which can be understood and turned back into a picture again by any heraldic student. Thus ' Papworth ' is arranged according to the heraldic description of the arms and an entry there will tell you which families used a particular coat of arms, whereas Burke's *General Armory* will tell you which arms were used by a particular family. ' Papworth ' does not include the crests but this is remedied in many ways by the extensive series of plates of crests arranged in ' ordinary ' order which forms the second volume of Fairbairn's *Book of Crests* (1905).

There are hundreds of books on heraldry but I have always found *Intelligible Heraldry* by C. and A. Lynch-Robinson (1948) a useful introduction which looks upon the subject in a practical way, and A. C. Fox-Davies' *Complete Guide to Heraldry* (1969) will answer most of the other questions. The special position in Scotland is described in Sir Thomas Innes of Learney's *Scots Heraldry* (1956). The recently founded Heraldry Society has done much to popularize the subject in general, particularly through its quarterly magazine *Coat of Arms*. Their address is 59 Gordon Square, London, W.C.1, where they maintain a Library for the use of members.

Heraldic ancestors may be expensive to trace, for you may never know how authentic they are unless you consult the appropriate heraldic authority, but despite the fees you and your ancestors will have paid there is still the delusion that you have the answer to that interesting question ' What shall be done to the man whom the king delighteth to honour? '

CHAPTER ELEVEN

Scotland, Ireland, and Englishmen Abroad

SCOTLAND and Ireland present somewhat contrasting features for the genealogist. In both, the main series of records, parish registers, wills and census, were called into central repositories, but that for Ireland was almost completely destroyed in 1922 and, as a result, genealogical research in Ireland is probably more difficult than in most other countries.

Ireland

Registration of births, marriages and deaths in Ireland started in 1864 and covers all Ireland up to 1921 the records being in the care of the Registrar General, Custom House, Dublin, who also holds those for the Republic of Ireland from that date to the present day, the fee for a search and certificate by post being 10s. 6d. In Northern Ireland the Registrar General, Fermanagh House, Ormeau Avenue, Belfast, has similar records since 1922. About one-third of the Parish Registers of Ireland survived the 1922 disaster, either not having been sent in or surviving in transcript form, mostly in the hands of the various incumbents. The Catholic registers which had not been collected, have thus also survived, but do not usually begin earlier than 1820. The Marriage Licences also were destroyed but abstracts of those from the Prerogative Court of Armagh and some other courts are preserved at the Genealogical Office, Dublin Castle, whilst others are at the Public Record Office, Dublin. Those from the Consistory Court of Dublin up to 1858 have been published in the Reports of the Deputy Keeper of the Irish Records.

The lack of registers is supplemented to a certain extent also by Monumental Inscriptions, many of which have been printed in the *Journal of the Irish Memorials Association*, and by notices in Irish newspapers of which there are runs from the eighteenth century in the National Library of Ireland, Dublin, and the British Museum Newspaper Library at Colindale.

Like the Prerogative Court of Canterbury in England the Prerogative Court of Armagh in Ireland had jurisdiction throughout the country before 1858. Wills proved therein were abstracted before destruction by Sir William Betham, 1536–1800, and these abstracts are at the Public Record Office, Dublin, pedigrees from them annotated by successive generations of heralds being at the Genealogical Office, Dublin Castle, the home of the Chief Herald of Ireland. A printed index of testators was issued by Sir Arthur Vicars in 1897. Many of the other destroyed Wills survive only in the form of printed indexes but copies, abstracts and Probate Copies are being collected by the Irish Record Office and an Index of those in the Genealogical Office was published by the Irish Manuscripts Commission in 1947 (No. 17 of *Analecta Hibernica*). Miss P. B. Eustace who edited this latter volume has edited two volumes (1954 and 1956) of Wills registered in the Registry of Deeds, Dublin, covering the period 1708–85, and also, in conjunction with Miss O. C. Goodbody, a volume of abstracts of Wills taken from the records of the Society of Friends (1957), all for the Irish Manuscripts Commission. Irish Wills between 1858 and 1904 are mostly missing but are complete from then to the present day.

The Registry of Deeds in Henrietta Street, Dublin, just mentioned, contains registered copies of transactions relating to land throughout Ireland. The series begins in 1708 and contains many wills and marriage settlements, is fairly well indexed, but none of it, apart from the Wills, has appeared in print.

Irish genealogy having special difficulties the guidance of the Irish Genealogical Research Society, 82 Eaton Square, London, S.W.1, may be helpful. It has published the *Irish Genealogist* since 1937, and Rosemary ffolliott's *A Simple Guide to Irish Genealogy* in 1966.

Scotland

In Scotland registration of Births, Deaths and Marriages began in 1855, and the records are in the custody of the Registrar General, New Register House, Edinburgh, 2, a search and certificate by post costing 8s. A general search can be made personally for a fee of £1 10s.

As mentioned earlier the ancient Parish Registers of the Church of Scotland are now all collected at the New Register House and there is a published list, *Detailed List of Old Parochial Registers of Scotland* (1872), which contains information as to the parishes for which registers exist and the years they cover. Most do not begin until the eighteenth century.

At the New Register House also are deposited the Census Records for 1841, 1851, 1861, 1871, 1881 and 1891 and the Registrar will supply certified extracts at 10s. for each particular search.

Two indispensable guides to Scottish research are Margaret Stuart's *Scottish Family History* (1930) and Livingstone's *Guide to the Public Records of Scotland* (1905). The Public Records are preserved in H.M. General Register House, Edinburgh, 2, and contain the Commissariot Court Records including all the Testaments (i.e. Wills) proved before 1823. These latter date from 1514 and indexes to all of them before 1800 have been published over a number of years by the Scottish Record Society. Wills proved in Scotland between 1823 and 1876 are mostly in the custody of the various sheriff clerks but since 1876 they have been centralized at the Record Office and an index published annually.

The Court of the Lord Lyon is the College of Arms for Scotland. Situated at the General Register House it has complete jurisdiction in the granting of arms and registering of pedigrees in Scotland. The present Lord Lyon, Sir Thomas Innes of Learney, has written an excellent work *Scots Heraldry* (1956) and another on *The Tartans of the Clans and Families of Scotland* (1958). A list of all the arms registered before 1901 comprises Sir James Balfour Paul's *An Ordinary of Arms in the Lyon Register* (1903), and he also compiled *The Scots Peerage* (8 vols. and index, 1904–14) which contains details of the collaterals and antecedents of all Scottish peers.

Again, Membership of the Scottish Genealogy Society, 21 Howard Place, Edinburgh, 3, which has published the *Scottish Genealogist* since 1954, may be of value to those interested.

Englishmen Abroad

English people leaving these Islands have left little record of their actual departure. There are practically no passenger lists before the second quarter of the last century except for those

forcibly taken as convicts (in the Public Record Office). Those
going to America are usually of greatest interest, regular emigration having started early in the seventeenth century, and those
lists of passengers which have appeared in print are detailed in
A Bibliography of Ship Passenger Lists 1538–1825 (New York
Public Library, 1963), some of the earlier ones being actually
indexed into C. E. Banks and E. E. Brownell's *Topographical
Dictionary of 2885 English emigrants to New England* 1620–1650
(1957).

Later emigrants to places abroad are often much more difficult
to trace unless some event, such as a birth, marriage or death of a
member of the family is known to have taken place in this
country since registration began and prior to emigration. Sometimes the will of the emigrant mentions relatives in England that
will help to identify his place of origin, or he may have married
here before emigrating and thus be found in Boyd's Marriage
Index. If an emigrant's place of origin cannot be found in this
way, the usual procedure is to abstract all the Wills of the same
surname proved in the Prerogative Court of Canterbury for about
50 years either side of the date of emigration in the hope of
finding some mention of him or a known member of his family.
If he himself still held property in England then his will should
be found in this court or the Prerogative Court of York.

A special index of those who were born or died at sea
(1837–75) is kept at Somerset House and applications for searches
should be made at the ' Marriage ' counter there. This is one of
several ' Miscellaneous Returns ' which include also registers of
births, marriages and deaths in the Army (including the South
African and both World Wars). Another of greater general
interest is the return of births, deaths and marriages of British
Subjects in Foreign Countries made by Consuls and the Administrators of British Protectorates. These range from Moscow to
Brazil and from Pekin to Rome and are all listed in the Appendix
to *Abstracts of Arrangements Respecting Registration of Births,
Marriages and Deaths in the United Kingdom and other
Countries of the British Commonwealth of Nations and in the
Irish Republic* (Registrar General, 1952), where also will be found
a list of similar returns made to the London Diocesan Registry of
baptisms, marriages and burials by English chaplains in foreign
places licensed by the Bishop of London. The records have

recently been transferred from the Diocesan Registry to the Guildhall Library, London, E.C.2, which has published a revised list of them (1967).

The above *Abstracts of Arrangements etc.* gives details of registration throughout the Commonwealth, and is indispensable, very full details being given in each case.   Births, deaths and marriages of English persons in India since 1698 are recorded at the India Office Library, Commonwealth Relations Office, 197 Blackfriars Road, London, S.E.1, and the *Guide to the India Office Records* by W. Foster (1920) should be consulted.   For Australia, which is well documented from early times, H. J. Rumsey's article in the *Genealogists' Magazine* (vol. 8, p. 135) is invaluable and the Australian Society of Genealogists, History House, 8 Young Street, Sydney, has done much valuable work in indexing records both here and in Australia.   It has published *The Australian Genealogist* (now called *Descent*), since 1933.

Registration in the Commonwealth often gives much more information than our own system but emigrants who moved across the world in search of a new life have often not left a great deal by which their origins can be identified, in certain cases, perhaps, it not being in their interest to do so.

Conclusion

T HE READER who has followed me this far will have noticed that it is impossible to generalize when speaking of family history because each family has its own special problems. To take one family and use it as an example immediately leads to difficulties as it would probably need only some of the sources mentioned in this book for its unravelling, and would thus not give a good picture of the sources for pedigree tracing in general. At the other extreme an annotated bibliography of genealogy would be very useful but not make particularly interesting reading, or explain the various stages of the research.

I hope that I have been able to steer a middle course between these two, giving sufficient explanation and bibliography at the same time. The earlier chapters of this book will apply to most families of English descent, but you will have to pick and choose in the rest for sources which may be applicable to your particular problem. You will soon come to realize that the difficulties you encounter are nearly always connected with the movement of your ancestors from one place to another and any record which may give a clue to the place of origin of your earliest known ancestor should be particularly studied whether it be will or marriage licence, settlement certificate or poll book entry.

There is no exhaustive text-book of genealogical method, but the three volumes so far published of D. E. Gardner's and F. Smith's *Genealogical Research in England and Wales* (U.S.A., 1956–1965) may be found of considerable value. The history of genealogical studies in England is outlined in A. R. Wagner's *English Genealogy* (1960), a fascinating book which has much to say on the possibilities of ancestor hunting, illustrated with some good examples. It also has an extensive bibliography in its foot-notes which may lead one to other sources.

The possibilities are, of course, not limited to your own male line. When an insurmountable problem arises you have always your female lines to trace. Members of the Society of Genealogists are asked to try and fill in a form showing their sixteen great-great-grandparents, and you can extend this idea to thirty-two, sixty-four, or more, to your heart's content; a special book, *Family Tree Record*, having been designed to record up to seven generations of ancestors on all sides. You can, on the other hand, limit your searches to the female line only and trace your mother's mother's mother, etc., as far as possible, a most difficult under-taking as the surname changes in each generation.

In all this I am presuming that you will undertake the work yourself. Only then will you be able to appreciate the difficulties involved and enjoy the excitement of solving a problem by your own ingenuity and detective work. There is no thrill in finding a pedigree of your family in a printed book but the slow piecing together of clues and information is a fascinating task, which, once you have started, you will find difficult to lay aside. In cases of particular difficulty you may have to enlist the help of a pro-fessional genealogist and if you are far away from London or the place where your ancestors lived there may be other problems that a record searcher can help with. Occasional assistance of this nature should not be too expensive and a fresh approach to the subject is often valuable as clues may be revealed which do not, at first sight, seem important to the amateur.

I must end with one word of warning. The spelling of surnames only became standardized with the growth of education in the last century and the ' y ' or the ' e ' in our names, about which we may be so particular, made little difference 150 years ago when, in a country parish, perhaps only the parson could write and might baptise one of your children Smith one year, another Smythe the next. The great George Villiers, indeed, appears in the parish registers of Kirkby Moorside, Yorkshire (1687), as ' Georges vilaus Lord dooke of bookingham ', so who are we to complain?

Appendix

SPECIMEN CERTIFICATES AND PARISH REGISTER ENTRIES

_____ _____ *George William Peters* of _____ *the* Parish

_____ *of Weston* _____

and *Annie Amelia Spinks* _____ of *this* Parish

___ *Minor* _____

were married in this _____ *Church* _____ by _____ *Licence* _____ with Consent of

her parents _____ this _____ *third* _____ Day of

December _____ in the Year One Thousand eight hundred and _____ *Nine*

By me _____ *G. T. Smith* *Rector* _____

This Marriage was solemnised between us
⎰ *George Wm Peters*
⎱ *Annie Amelia Spinks*

In the Presence of _____ *John Williams* _____

_____ *L. Trattle* _____

No.567

1. Form of Marriage entry to be found in all
Parish Registers between 1754 and 1837.

BAPTISMS solemnized in the Parish of *Southcombe* in the County of *Hampshire* in the Year 18 _14_

When Baptised	Child's Christian Name	Parents Name — Christian	Parents Name — Surname	Abode	Quality, Trade, or Profession	By whom the Ceremony was performed
April 4th No. 817	*William son of*	*William and Anne*	*Assur*	*Southcombe*	*Labourer*	*Geo: Thomas*
11th No. 818	*Alfred son of*	*George and Mary*	*Hayes*	*do*	*Sojourners*	*Geo: Thomas*
May 3rd No. 819	*Edward son of*	*Edward and Alice*	*Smiley*	*do*	*Labourer*	*Geo: Thomas*
10th No. 820	*Joan base daughter of*	*Mary*	*Barr*	*do*	*Spinster*	*Wm Smythe Curate*
19th No. 821	*Samuel son of*	*John and Mary*	*Clegg*	*Hill End*	*Carpenter*	*Geo: Thomas*
July 2nd No. 822	*Margaret daughter of*	*Henry and Rose*	*Wray*	*Southcombe*	*Joiner*	*Geo: Thomas*

2. Form of Baptismal Register to be found in all Parishes between 1813 and 1837, and still in use at present time.

BURIALS in the Parish of _Southcombe_

in the County of _Hampshire_ in the Year 18 _13_

Name	Abode	When buried	Age	By whom the Ceremony was performed
Thomas Parker No. 657	Southcombe	December 10th 1813	2 months	Geo: Thomas
William Hall No. 658	Southcombe	December 13th	69	Geo: Thomas
Daniel Assur No. 659	Southcombe	30th	25	Geo: Thomas Vicar
Edward Barry No. 660	Crouch Lane	March 4th 1814	67	Geo: Thomas
Rose Barr No. 661	Southcombe	16th	3 days	Geo: Thomas
Samuel Porter No. 662	Hill End	24th	63	Geo: Thomas

3. Form of Burial Register to be found in all Parishes between 1813 and 1837, and still in use at present **time.**

BIRTH in the Sub-district of _Kennington_ _Ist._ in the _County_ of _London_

No.	When and where born	Name, if any	Sex	Name, and surname of father	Name, surname, and maiden surname of mother	Occupation of father	Signature, description, and residence of informant	When registered	Signature of Registrar
476	Ninth May 1856 38 The Grove South Lambeth	John William	Boy	Charles Henry Smith	Isobel Smith formerly Williams	Shipping clerk	I. Smith, Mother, 38 The Grove South Lambeth	Twenty fifth June 1856	W.H. Edwards Registrar

MARRIAGE solemnized at _The Register Office_ in the _District_ of _St. Saviour Southwark_ in the _County_ of _London_

No.	When married	Name and surname	Age	Condition	Rank or profession	Residence at the time of marriage	Father's name and surname	Rank or profession of father
307	28th April 1879	John William Smith	22	Bachelor	Baker	5 Collinson Street	Charles Henry Smith	Shipping clerk
		Mary Ellen Jones	20	Spinster	Servant	10 Bath Street	William Jones	Auctioneer

Married in the _Register Office_ according to the of the _by Certificate_ before me

This marriage was solemnized between us { John William Smith / Mary Ellen Jones } in the presence of us, { Francis Jones / Abigail Smith } W.P. Williams Registrar / H.C. Phillips Supt. Registrar.

DEATH in the Sub-district of _St. Saviour Southwark_ in the _County_ of _London_

No.	When and where died	Name and surname	Sex	Age	Occupation	Cause of death	Signature, description, and residence of informant	When registered	Signature of Registrar
964	Fourteenth December 1915 at 5 Collinson Street	John William Smith	Male	57 years	Baker	Tuberculosis Certified by J. Langston, L.R.C.P.	Henry Smith son of deceased Present at death 5 Collinson Street	Seventeenth December 1914	E. Finlay Registrar

4. Typical birth, marriage and death certificates from Somerset House. The form of these certificates has not changed since they were introduced in 1837.

Index

Administrations, 28
America, 69
Apprenticeships, 37
Army records, 38, 69
Association Oath Rolls, 45
Attorneys, 39
Australia, 70

Baptists, 33
Baronets, 40
Biographical Dictionaries, 40
Bishops Transcripts, 24
British Museum Library, 45
Bunhill Fields, 34

Census Returns:
  England & Wales, 17
  Scotland, 68
Chancery Records, 43
Chaplains Returns, 69
Charter Rolls, 44
Churchwardens' Accounts, 26
Clergy, 39
Close Rolls, 44
College of Arms, 60
Commonwealth, 68
Congregationalists, 33
Consular Returns, 69
County Record Offices, 55
Court of Chivalry, 60
Court of Lord Lyon, 62

Diaries, 40

Diocesan Record Offices, 57
Directories, 40
Domesday Ancestors, 11
Dr. Williams' Library, 34

Enclosure Awards, 56

Feet of Fines, 44
Funeral Certificates, 64

Genealogists, Society of, 50
Gentleman's Magazine, 47
Grants of Arms, 62

Harleian Manuscripts, 47
Hearth Tax, 45
Heraldry Society, 65
Huguenots, 35

India, 70
Inns of Court, 39
Inquisitions post mortem, 43
Inventories, 30
Ireland, 62, 66
Irish Genealogical Research Society,
  67

Jews, 22, 33, 35

Knights, 40

Land Registry, 41
Land Tax Assessments, 56

77